FORCES  INFLUENCE

FORCES OF INFLUENCE

HOW
EDUCATORS
CAN LEVERAGE
RELATIONSHIPS
TO IMPROVE
PRACTICE

FRED ENDE
and
MEGHAN EVERETTE

Scott, to be
Excited to be
Cohort B with you!

Meghan
Everette

ASCD

Alexandria, Virginia USA

1703 N. Beauregard St. • Alexandria, VA 22311-1714 USA
Phone: 800-933-2723 or 703-578-9600 • Fax: 703-575-5400
Website: www.ascd.org • E-mail: member@ascd.org
Author guidelines: www.ascd.org/write

Ranjit Sidhu, *Executive Director and CEO;* Stefani Roth, *Publisher;* Genny Ostertag, *Director, Content Acquisitions;* Susan Hills, *Senior Acquisitions Editor;* Julie Houtz, *Director, Book Editing & Production;* Miriam Calderone, *Editor;* Judi Connelly, *Senior Art Director;* Donald Ely, *Associate Art Director;* Cynthia Stock, *Typesetter;* Kelly Marshall, *Interim Manager, Production Services;* Trinay Blake, *E-Publishing Specialist;* Isel Pizarro, *Senior Production Specialist*

All web links in this book are correct as of the publication date below but may have become inactive or otherwise modified since that time. If you notice a deactivated or changed link, please e-mail books@ascd.org with the words "Link Update" in the subject line. In your message, please specify the web link, the book title, and the page number on which the link appears.

PAPERBACK ISBN: 978-1-4166-2873-6   ASCD product #120009   n2/20
PDF E-BOOK ISBN: 978-1-4166-2874-3; see Books in Print for other formats.
Quantity discounts are available: e-mail programteam@ascd.org or call 800-933-2723, ext. 5773, or 703-575-5773. For desk copies, go to www.ascd.org/deskcopy.

Library of Congress Cataloging-in-Publication Data

Names: Ende, Fred, author. | Everette, Meghan, author.
Title: Forces of influence : how educators can leverage relationships to improve practice / Fred Ende, Meghan Everette.
Description: Alexandria, Virginia : ASCD, 2020. | Includes bibliographical references and index. | Summary: "The authors introduce four "forces," or levels, of influence that educators can use to leverage relationships to support one another's practice and effect positive change"—Provided by publisher.
Identifiers: LCCN 2019044663 (print) | LCCN 2019044664 (ebook) | ISBN 9781416628736 (paperback) | ISBN 9781416628743 (pdf)
Subjects: LCSH: Teachers—Professional relationships—United States. | Educators—Professional relationships—United States. | Educational change—United States.
Classification: LCC LB1775.2 .E524 2020 (print) | LCC LB1775.2 (ebook) | DDC 371.1—dc23
LC record available at https://lccn.loc.gov/2019044663
LC ebook record available at https://lccn.loc.gov/2019044664

30 29 28 27 26 25 24 23 22 21 20   1 2 3 4 5 6 7 8 9 10 11 12

FORCES OF INFLUENCE

HOW EDUCATORS CAN LEVERAGE RELATIONSHIPS TO IMPROVE PRACTICE

Acknowledgments

This book sprang from the kernel of an idea I had more than three years ago. The transformation of this wisp of a thought into the tangible book you have in your hands didn't happen in a vacuum. I truly owe tremendous thanks to hundreds; the few I mention here had a significant impact on pulling, pushing, shoving, and nudging me and this book to the finish line.

I've never had the fortune to cowrite anything longer than a blog post before. Meghan was precisely the superstar coauthor who showed me just how valuable (and fun) it is to write with someone else. Susan Hills and Miriam Calderone were precisely the types of editors needed to bring this book to fruition. They are experts in using the Forces of Influence, to be sure, and their feedback and guidance helped us turn this book into an engaging and practical read.

ASCD as a whole has continued to serve as a resource for my growth. Providing me with the opportunity to write about this work and design professional learning on the topic helped fully actualize this idea. My critical friends group, "The BFFs," provided tremendous assistance throughout the writing process on both the book and everything else going on in my life. Dr. Marla Gardner served as a steadfast supporter of this work and has been a mentor in all things education (and life), including the ideas herein. I also want to thank the entire PNW BOCES organization; it is phenomenal to work for an agency that promotes and supports the growth of leaders and learners in all directions.

My parents, sister, and other family members did precisely what they are supposed to do: provide me with the most flattering feedback possible, often unsubstantiated and always appreciated. To Laurie, Sydney, and Ardyn: thank you for standing by my side as I wrote, standing in front of me when I needed to rebalance and take a break, and standing behind me when I needed to be pushed (or shoved) to move the work forward. I couldn't ask for anything more.

—Fred Ende

I don't know that I ever truly experienced writer's block until I tried to put into words my immense gratitude for the opportunity to write this book.

I am eternally grateful to Fred for the well-placed pull three years ago that started us on the path to writing this book. ASCD has provided me with innumerable opportunities to develop as a leader, to write, and to share my work with others, while the ASCD Emerging Leaders have been a constant source of support and inspiration, personally and professionally, throughout the process of writing this book. Editors Susan Hills and Miriam Calderone provided insight and guidance while being thoughtful and dedicated cheerleaders from the proposal stage through publication.

I don't know how to properly thank those who were on the receiving end of my stressed-out texts, who provided calm perspective, career advice, quality gossip, procrastination suggestions in the form of binge-worthy shows and can't-put-down books, or just a laugh when I got overwhelmed by writing or life. "The BFFs," LAUs, and Lady Bosses ground me and keep me giggling. My parents have been unyielding supporters, letting me know I'm loved no matter what. They have always known when to push, pull, nudge, or shove—or when to dump water over my head when I get too big for my britches. Shannon is always there to talk through an idea or blame the camera angle, as only a sister and best friend can. To Bridger and Taplin, thank you for the coffee dates, unprompted hugs, and comic relief. I'm prouder of you both than you'll ever know. To Justin, thank you for never doubting my ability to take on the world and allowing me time to write, work, and explore my passions without reservation. I'm lucky you decided to come waste your time with me. And to Boomer, who spent more writing and editing hours by my side than any other, thank you for always keeping my toes toasty warm.

—*Meghan Everette*

Introduction

First of all, hi, we're Fred and Meghan. We've spent the last few years researching, reflecting on, and reacting to situations that have confronted us in both our professional roles as director of curriculum and instruction and mathematics coach, respectively, and our personal lives. We've looked at their connection to the people we work with, the processes we engage in, and the products we create. Based on our experiences and those of others, this book is all about how educators can more effectively use relationships to support one another's practice and push for stronger positive outcomes for all learners. It's about how we can most effectively influence others to bring about needed change. So with this introduction in place, which is the start of any good relationship, we're glad to meet you, and we hope you'll read on.

We thought we couldn't talk about relationships without explaining how we became coauthors for this book in which relationships feature so prominently. It was a dark and stormy night. . . .

But, no, really, we met at a professional leadership conference some years ago. Through both professional networking at the conference and more personal networking among friends, a small group of like-minded individuals decided that we enjoyed one another's professional insights and personal commentary so much that we should keep in touch after the conference. Through a social media app, a group of about 12 people continued discussing their professional lives and interests. As time wore on, this group whittled down to six. By checking in daily and listening to one another's needs, our group became close critical friends professionally as well as personally. Through increased trust and respect, a number of us have collaborated on presentations, writing projects, and committee work.

On the basis of shared interest and a presentation that we facilitated a number of years ago, both of us felt that we had the interest and capacity to put together a book on relationship building and leveraging relationships to do great work. And the rest is history (or not quite history, but you get the idea).

A Look at the Book

It's helpful to start out by describing the lay of the land. In Chapter 1, "Influence: It's All About Relationships," we explain how relationships form—and how to leverage them to get things done. In Chapter 2, "Give to Get," we talk about the transactional nature of relationships and how leverage and influence come into play. Chapter 3, "The Forces of Influence," will introduce you to the Forces of Influence Leadership Matrix, which will help you nail your influence style.

Chapters 4 through 7 investigate each of the four forces we can use to influence change: the pull, the push, the shove, and the nudge. Quite coincidentally, we title these chapters "The Pull" (Chapter 4); "The Push" (Chapter 5); "The Shove" (Chapter 6); and "The Nudge" (Chapter 7).

But what happens, you may ask, when a force you've chosen doesn't result in the desired change? No worries; we've got your back. We address this issue in the last two chapters of the book. In Chapter 8, "Stacking the Forces," we show you how you can apply an additional force when the first one hasn't worked, and in Chapter 9, "When Forces Succeed and Fail," we look at how forces can go bad, but how you can recover.

A quick note: at the end of each chapter, we provide questions to spur reflection and action taking. You can explore the group questions through protocol use or open conversation. As for the tools shared in the book, and there are many—worksheets, self-assessments, templates, and more—you can find downloadable copies in our resource folder at http://tiny.cc/ForcesofInfluence. We also offer several in-depth tools in the Appendices located at the end of this book.

So now, read on!

1

Influence:
It's All About
Relationships

As you begin this chapter, you're likely hoping for ideas, tips, and tools to promote the relationships you've spent time crafting so you can continue to get the good work done. And you might be wondering, in fairness, if starting with a look at relationships is taking two steps backward. After all, you may already understand the value of relationships, and you may already be a leader who focuses on the interactions you have with others.

Those are valid points, but the goal of this first chapter isn't simply to convince you that relationships are important. Rather, it's to understand how relationships form and what enables them to thrive or falter. This, in turn, will help provide context as we explore how to leverage relationships to get things done; it will also help explain why certain Forces of Influence (the pulls, pushes, shoves, and nudges we will explore throughout this book) work and don't work in certain situations. It's just as important for the artist to have the right easel and paints as it is to actually know how to paint the

picture. Therefore, before we strategize about leveraging relationships, it pays to remind ourselves of how and why the relationships
we engage in daily flourish—or don't.

Why Relationships Are Important

When we consider the essential things in life, the backbone behind
our actions and feelings, relationships are at the forefront. We can
pare down why we work and what we love to our connections with
others and to the thoughts, feelings, and needs that drive and sustain those relationships. If relationships are at the heart of our "why,"
then it follows that relationships are paramount to our work and
personal lives.

Research tells us that healthy relationships are key to healthy liv-
ing. Those who struggle in their relationships often suffer the same
negative side effects as those who smoke or who suffer from obe-
sity, such as depression, decreased immune function, and high blood
pressure (Kreitzer, 2016). Good relationships have mood-boosting
effects, and people who have healthy social relationships have a
50 percent higher survival rate than those who don't (Holt-Lunstad,
Smith, & Layton, 2010). Above and beyond these very real health
benefits, good relationships become even more necessary and powerful when it comes to influencing others.

Consider the common workplace dilemma. When tasked with
overcoming an obstacle, from whom are you most likely to solicit
advice? Likely, you'll go to your closest coworkers, friends, or mentors, those who have a track record of giving valuable counsel. Even
those with whom you worked previously are more likely sources of
feedback than mere acquaintances. When someone you don't know

well jumps in to give you advice, however well intentioned, how likely are you to listen? We tend to avoid opening up our personal circles of trust and often become antagonistic toward ideas that come from outside an existing relationship.

Power in relationships fluctuates with the types of decisions being made. For instance, you might wield great influence over your friend's vacation choice but far less influence over his or her financial plans. And although power isn't always synonymous with influence, a certain degree of power is necessary to effect change in others. That power comes as a direct result of the relationship forged. In 1983, Huston suggested a theory called *power in relationships,* which suggests that power is the ability to exert influence and that this influence depends on what each person in the relationship is thinking, feeling, and doing at the time. As you might have noticed in your own personal and professional relationships, the power of influence from a friend, a relationship in which you feel comfortable and secure, is often better received and more likely to be acted on than influence coming from someone you know less well.

Fostering relationships, then, not only supports your own well-being but also smooths the way to exert influence over others for positive change. That being the case, how do we build and sustain such relationships?

Building relationships differs from networking, something we all increasingly find ourselves engaged in. Although networking is often a one-and-done experience to amass potential connections, relationships are much more complicated; they require energy and intention for the long haul. Shelley Zalis (2018), chief executive officer of the Female Quotient, says it well: "Networking is nine to five; relationships are forever" (para. 9).

The Stages of Relationships

On the basis of our work in this area, we see four stages in relationship growing.

Introduction Stage

In this stage, potential relationship builders meet. This might involve a face-to-face, verbal, or written meeting or a hybrid version of these. During this phase, those involved are listening to what is and isn't being said. Often it's just as much about assessing the transactional value of the relationship that is forming (more on this later) as it is about assessing the value of the content being discussed. For the relationship to move beyond this stage, those involved have to see the value of both continued interaction and, down the line, potential quid pro quo. (Set aside your possible discomfort with that term and, for now, just know that every relationship forms for a reason.) Networking goes through this stage as well, but it often never advances further.

Testing Stage

Every relationship requires a large amount of energy to build and sustain (even the ones we're born into). To determine whether we should invest that energy, we need to test the beginning of a relationship to see whether it can withstand simple stressors and whether it can lead us to improve the work we do with others and ourselves. The testing stage can be short or long, depending on the desired scope of the relationship.

For example, the testing stage for a fellow student who lives two doors down from you on a college dorm floor would be shorter than that for a potential life partner or spouse. This stage often involves probing questions that get to the beliefs and values of those involved, as well as activities that might provide insight into whether the relationship partner will or won't carry his or her own weight when relationships build.

Trusting Stage

Once a level of trust has been established, doors open up, guards are let down, and relationships take on more meaning and can accomplish greater things. The trusting stage can be somewhat lengthy as those involved share personal information, continue to meet and work together, and show who they really are. Because members of the relationship feel supported and cared for by their partners, they can make mistakes from time to time without fearing that those blunders will result in the breakdown of the relationship.

Interestingly enough, it's also here that the direction of a relationship is charted. Will the relationship move beyond a friendly one to a more intimate one? Work by Arthur Aron and colleagues (Goodwin, 2018) identified a series of 36 questions (Jones, 2015) that may be asked during this stage that can help direct how a relationship grows. For example, "For what in your life do you feel most grateful?" or "If you could wake up tomorrow having gained one quality or ability, what would it be?" Such questions are worth exploring for the impact they can have on a relationship's direction.

Bonded Stage

In relationships that reach this stage, members are tied tightly together. They know enough about the others in the relationship to identify strengths and weaknesses, and they're comfortable enough with their place in the relationship to be honest, open, and, for lack of a better word, themselves. Once in the bonded stage, we have to do three things to sustain our relationships:

- **We need to check in.** All productive relationships require regular check-ins. "Regular" will depend on the strength of the bond that holds the relationship together. Without checking in, no relationship will be sustained. Checking in can be as simple as making a phone call, sending an e-mail or a text, visiting someone, or sending a card. Some methods of checking in won't work for certain relationships. The good news? By the time a relationship has reached the bonded stage, members tend to know what works and what doesn't. Check-ins are really the most important step to sustaining relationships; they're a must in the sustaining toolbox.

- **We need to add fuel.** Relationships are built on energy. It takes energy to form and sustain them, and it consumes quite a bit of emotional energy when they fall apart. To sustain relationships, we have to add fuel. We can do this in many different ways, such as embarking on a new experience together, adding a new person to the relationship, or trying to solve a challenging problem. Negative circumstances, such as a death in the family or losing a job, can also add fuel, and those circumstances, too, can strengthen relationship bonds. We need to add fuel to keep relationships moving, and we have to do so consistently.

- **We need to self-reflect.** To determine whether we want to keep a relationship going, we need to ask ourselves what our true investment is in it. Is it worth our time and energy? What will it take to keep things moving? How often we consider these questions depends on how important the relationship is to us and how regularly we add fuel and check-ins. The point is, relationships are always two-way streets. We have to continually think about them to make sure we keep them going (or don't).

Fostering Good Relationships

According to research, various structural foundations can help foster relationships. In his work on networking, Baker (1994) maintains that working with an adversarial approach doesn't lead to success the way building on consensus and mutual interest can. For example, enabling people to get the tools they need to work effectively can build lasting relationships. Research from Gratton and Erickson (2007) on relationship building in the business world also provides insight. Some actionable steps include the following:

- **Create teams where some relationships already exist.** Building on existing relationships supports relationship development. If you're working in a team structure, pulling in a known entity can help everyone feel comfortable and allied from the start. Think of this as a double date. The pressure of building a relationship is lessened by having a friend around. The same thing can be true when building professional relationships.
- **Provide time and space for building social relationships.** Gratton and Erickson offer the example of the headquarters of the Royal Bank of Scotland, which was designed with communal areas, atriums, and eating spaces to encourage the

formation of social relationships among employees. Although few of us are in a position to redesign the layout of a building, creating social opportunity within workspaces is possible. Push tables together for more collaborative space, or encourage lunching together. Be intentionally visible before or after school, and open conversation with others. Small moves make big gains in relationship building.

- **Be task oriented initially and build the relationship over time.** When relationships are not yet bonded, staying task oriented can foster collaborative work. Gratton and Erickson (2007) suggest leaving the path to finishing a task less well defined; this fosters the need for people to work together and build relationships within the framework of that task. Baker (1994) adds that forming groups around the interests of those involved helps build stronger teams and stronger relationships.

The magic of connection also plays a role in the process. Think of building a relationship as learning to read. You learn the basics of letters, sounds, and word formation, all while developing vocabulary outside your focus on learning to read. At some point, some connection you make takes sounding out words, determining context, and comprehending to a whole new level. And that's just how it is with relationships. You can work through the stages and societal norms of crafting a relationship, you can have the standard meeting over coffee and camaraderie at the water cooler, yet there's a certain amount of connection that draws us closer in some relationships than in others.

Ibarra and Hunter (2007) cite three interdependent forms of connecting—operational, personal, and strategic—that they looked at through the lens of networking. We contend that their work also applies to the more complex nature of relationship building. *Operational relationships* are focused on accomplishing work and are based on who is needed to execute a task. *Personal relationships* are cultivated to help achieve one's future goals, but the players are less defined because you never know to whom those contacts might connect you in the future. *Strategic relationships* are focused on making connections for future stakeholder support but are less personal in nature. The managers studied didn't always readily understand the importance of building more personal relationships, but Ibarra and Hunter found that doing so leads to creating a safe space. And that safe space is where relationships become the foundation for allowing influence to happen.

Four Essential Keys to Relationship Building

Research overwhelmingly shows that listening, trust, respect, and collaboration are the four keys to building successful relationships. With the right percentage of each ingredient (which varies from relationship recipe to relationship recipe), we can build any successful relationship. If you experiment with the emphasis you place on each of these four ingredients, you'll eventually find the best recipe for that relationship. This trial-and-error approach is why relationship building has so many stages and is so complex (and why it often takes many tries to make the perfect cake).

Listening

Listening sets the stage for all other communication and relationship building to happen. Although people generally don't feel called on to improve their listening skills, the average person listens with only 25 percent efficiency (Huseman & Lahiff, 1981). Effective listening involves maintaining interest at a deeper level than simply taking in information and responding so the speaker knows you're listening. It's only true interest that enables relationships to grow and flourish beyond the early stages. Listening without the intent to respond or offer advice—listening to understand—goes against our problem-solving and "me first" society. To master effective listening, you have to actively practice the skill (Williams, 2004). The best listeners are empathetic, keep an open mind, pose significant questions, and don't become defensive (Holmes, 2017). Good listening sets the foundation for trust and respect to build.

Trust

Trust is of great value in our interactions with others, be those interactions personal or professional. According to Michelle and Dennis Reina of the Reina Trust Building Institute, "Business is conducted through relationships, and trust is the foundation of those relationships" (Reina & Reina, 2007, p. 36). Building trust is all about doing what we say we're going to do. When we make a promise or state a claim and then deliver on it, we prove our word is good. And when our word is good, it's more likely people can believe what we say will happen without worrying about whether it's actually going to happen or not. The Great Workplace model (Burchell & Robin, 2011) lists credibility, respect, and fairness—the basics of trust—as the foundations of an ideal working environment. How safe people feel relates directly to the level of trust they have in an organization, a leader, or a relationship.

Note that trust is earned over time, little by little. We've all experienced the over-sharer, that person who creates an awkward balance by sharing too personal an experience early on. Likewise, collegial relationships are most effective when members share professional challenges a little at a time and when they avoid being too blunt in expressing their opinions and challenging ideas. Trust takes time to develop.

Respect

A study (Porath, 2014) that included more than 20,000 employees worldwide found that no other factor has greater influence on employees than respect. When people feel respected, they are happier, experience greater fulfillment in their jobs, and are more likely to stay engaged. That said, respect can be one of the trickiest aspects of a relationship to develop. Respect is different for all people; it depends on culture, generation, gender, industry, and societal norms.

Darwall (1977) states there are two types of respect: recognition respect and appraisal respect. *Recognition respect* is the basic respect we should have for all human beings. It's a kind of moral obligation to treat others well. When we respect others, we let them be who they are, and we make sure we welcome all they bring to the table (although, in fairness, there's only so much potato salad you can bring to one table). This type of respect is pretty easy to showcase. We simply have to see the good in each and every person we encounter and value them for the person they currently are and not necessarily for the person we wish they would be. *Appraisal respect* means weighing another's qualities and finding him or her worthy. It's the kind of respect you work to earn in a relationship. So how can you cultivate appraisal respect? By listening and building trust, by being honest about what you're willing and unwilling to do, by engaging in active listening, and by being supportive in all you do. Respect is built over time through consistent and reliable interactions.

Collaboration

With respect well established, you can move on to productive collaboration. Relationships can only form if the opportunity to work together for the common good comes into play. We need collaboration to be in place if we're going to be effective at using relationships to influence and support others. The need to communicate effectively, cooperate, and be comfortable with an action "not going your way" are key tenets of successful collaboration.

Why is collaboration so important when it comes to relationship building? Because collaboration is about "doing," and when we "do" something together, we bond better. One of the best ways to foster a collaborative stance is to recognize that every idea is valuable. As Anthony Kim and Alexis Gonzales-Black discuss in their excellent book *The New School Rules* (2018), we can become better at learning, growing, and taking action if we adopt a "safe enough to try" mentality. This approach makes collaboration easier because it values proposals and experimentation rather than solutions, perfection, or consensus. Collaboration is always about focusing on key outcomes and using one another's strengths to achieve an overarching goal.

To keep our minds on these foundations, we've devised a Relationship Audit that you can use to reflect on your relationships with others (see Figure 1.1). It's simple, really. At the top, jot down the relationship you want to audit. Then fill in the activities or events that have occurred with this person (or people) over the last day, week, and month. Finally, consider the roles held. Were you a Giver?

Figure 1.1 **Relationship Audit**

The purpose of this tool is to help you gauge where your current relationships stand. It will help you determine whether you need to put additional work into sustaining those relationships or whether you can back off and focus on others.

Relationship to Review (include all people involved):

Length of Relationship Through Today (be specific):

Frequency of Contact with Relationship Participants Over the Last Week, Month, and Year:

Week	Month	Year

Relationship Roles Held Over the Last Year (be specific):

Giver	Taker	Wonderer

Do you need to put more work into this relationship? To answer this question,

- Reflect on the length of the relationship. Longer-term relationships can generally withstand less constant contact.

- Count how often you have contacted relationship participants. The higher the number of contacts, the better, and the less likely that you'll need to put more work into the relationship currently.

- Explore the ratio of roles held. If one person is occupying one role more often than others, this could indicate the need to strengthen the relationship by bringing balance to the roles.

A Taker? A Wonderer? (If you need additional clarification about what these roles entail, we expand on them below.)

When you've completed the audit, ask yourself two questions: (1) Have I been remiss in focusing on one of the four relationship foundations—listening, trust, respect, and collaboration—at the expense of another? (2) Did I do a great job building this relationship but a poor job sustaining it? (To answer this question, look at your frequency of contact data.) Relationship audits don't necessarily solve any of our relationship problems, but they do bring to light the fact that no relationship can exist in a vacuum; it takes work to build and sustain the connections we have.

The Roles We Play

So let's take stock. We've talked about why relationships tend to form, the different layers of relationship building, the ingredients for sustaining relationships, and the four building blocks of relationships. There's one last piece to discuss before moving on: the different roles we occupy when playing a part in relationships.

As we'll attempt to show over the course of this book, all relationships are transactional (well, almost all; there really isn't anything you can do about your crazy Aunt Jill). As we'll also attempt to show, there's nothing bad about coming to this realization.

The simple fact is this: we form the vast majority of relationships because we believe that we can give something to the other person (or people) in the relationship and that they, in turn, can give something to us. The "something" doesn't have to be a physical product. It can range from support, counseling, and love to a job, a written recommendation, or a brand-new car (we're game show fans here).

And regardless of whether the giving and taking involve something "holdable" or not, there are three roles we consistently play in relationships. Here they are, in no particular order (and note that over the course of a relationship, we're apt to switch these roles many, many times):

- **Giver:** When operating in this role, we're the ones completing the transaction for the other person or people. There's something we need to be giving to fulfill needs, whether it's affection, a sympathetic ear, or a peanut butter and jelly sandwich. When serving as a Giver, we're technically in control of where the relationship goes next. By fulfilling needs, we allow the relationship to move to the next transaction, where the roles may switch. If we don't fulfill the need, the relationship is likely to stay put and continue by virtue of the ingredients used to originally build it, or fall apart because it's difficult to sustain.
- **Taker:** The Taker in a relationship is simply that. It's the person or people who have needs that must be fulfilled and who "purchase" something from the Giver. This can be a monetary purchase, certainly, or it can be a different type of withdrawal, such as from a bank of emotions. Takers take something from others as a way of fulfilling needs, sometimes leaving Givers with less, and sometimes leaving them with more. For any relationship to grow and flourish, both these roles must always be present. As with the Giver, a Taker can sometimes overstay the role. Relationship participants who spend too much time in one of these roles can get burned out or can burn out the relationship.

- **Wonderer:** When relationships are starting out or when a relationship transaction has been completed, there's often a sense of the unknown regarding the next role to play. In these situations, relationship participants enter the Wonderer role, which is focused on identifying the next opportunity for those involved to support one another. For example, Meghan recently was the subject of a case study in teacher leadership. When the case study was finished, she and the interviewer entered the wondering stage, where their relationship going forward was unknown. Would the interviewer call on Meghan again? Would Meghan reach out and ask the interviewer to participate in her own study? Would they remain friends or colleagues, or go their separate ways? Participants can spend a substantial amount of time in this role; at this point, the effort that goes into sustaining the relationship is of the greatest importance.

In the next chapter, we'll shift to exploring the transactional nature of relationships in greater detail by looking at influence, its power, and why influence is necessary for all leaders and learners.

Questions for Self-Reflection
- Reflect on the four stages of relationship building. Select four relationships that you're currently involved in that would fit into each of the four stages. How are those relationships different? How are you continuing to build and sustain them?

Questions for Group Discussion
- When we think of the four building blocks for relationships (listening, trust, respect, and collaboration), which do we consider to be our greatest strength? Our biggest weakness? Why?
- Consider the fact that all relationships are transactional. What does this mean to us? Do we agree? Disagree? Why?

2

Give to Get

As we mentioned in Chapter 1, few relationships form in which a want or need doesn't play a role. This doesn't necessarily mean that the vast majority of relationships form with quid pro quo as a foundation. We can form relationships because we hope to give something or get something without any type of expectation in return. But in all fairness, a relationship formed in which all involved recognize they can support one another and hope to give to and gain from one another is much more good than bad.

We often consider anything tied to quid pro quo as being nefarious; the use of the phrase to highlight misconduct in the workplace, for instance, makes it difficult to appreciate a transactional view of relationships. However, if we can partition our thinking to remove the truly nasty cases of giving and taking, we can better understand that the ebb and flow of relationships often operate in a similar fashion to the buy and sell elements of supply and demand theory.

Think about your purchase of this book. Clearly something made you decide to want to own it, and there was at least an individual demand on your part to buy it. To obtain it, there had to be an adequate supply of the book. And as in a supply and demand scenario, you provided a service (a payment) to receive a different service (the delivery of the text).

Let's expand the idea of the transactional nature of supply and demand cultures to focus on a situation that a leader might encounter when working with a colleague. Let's say you have expertise in the area of integrating technology into instruction. Many of your colleagues seek you out to help them think about how to use technology in different ways. Because you believe in the merits of continuous improvement, you provide assistance whenever you can, and in return, your colleagues grow their practice. They hope to learn from you, and you hope that their growth in the area of technology use increases and that students will benefit (and your time was well spent). Both parties have expectations for what happens after the "transaction"; neither party leaves assuming the process is complete.

Leverage and Influence in Relationships

Because almost every relationship involves expectations on the part of everyone involved, it's only natural to see those relationships as transactional. But there's something else at play. In every relationship, leverage and influence play a tremendous role. What are these terms? How are they different? Let's investigate.

When we refer to *influence,* we're often talking about the ability of someone or something to change actions, ideas, or character. The amount of influence can be large or small; influence is more about the capacity to affect someone or something and less about a specific quantity. *Leverage* often refers to the ability to influence a person, product, or practice to the maximum. Much like a lever allows for greater exertion of force (influence), leverage occurs when a person applies influence to the full effect. Notice that we wrote "when a *person* applies influence to the full effect" as opposed to "when something applies influence to the full effect." Although products or ideas may influence us to make changes to our practice, leverage is something that only people can exert and, realistically, only consciously. We may not be aware of the influence we have on others, but we are aware of the leverage we put into practice.

To explore how these two terms come together, we call your attention to Figure 2.1, which shows an Influence Worksheet. You'll notice that Part I asks you to consider (1) when you've influenced others or been influenced, and (2) how you've used leverage or how leverage has been exerted on you. As we imagine you'll find, situations in which you use influence or leverage will be much easier to identify than those in which you've been influenced or someone else has used leverage to help you get somewhere. We would ask you to stop whatever you're doing and take a few minutes to complete Part I of the sheet now. We'll wait; we don't have anywhere else to be.

All set? Let's continue.

The purpose of Part I of the worksheet is twofold. (Don't think we've forgotten Part II; we'll ask you to fill that part out later on in this chapter.) We want you to become comfortable identifying when you use influence and leverage and when you're on the receiving end. Just as important, we want you to begin to feel just as comfortable using and exerting these relationship tools as being used by them. In fact, once we consider the positive ways that we can use influence and leverage, we can relax a bit when we pick up on the ways we've changed for the better because of the influence someone used on us.

In the case of writing this book, for instance, we were able to influence each other to explore many of these ideas through an

Figure 2.1 **Influence Worksheet**

This tool can help you explore your use of influence/leverage and reflect on when these have been used on you.

Part I: List specific instances of influence and leverage use. Use this list to reflect on yourself as an influencer/influencee and leverager/leveragee.

When Have I Exerted Influence?	When Have I Been Influenced?	When Have I Used Leverage?	When Have I Been Leveraged?

Part II: Identify some relationships you engage in and explore them in terms of the three Rs (role, resources, and respect). On the basis of these Rs, does the balance of influence/leverage make sense? Why or why not?

Relationship	Role	Resources	Respect

initial presentation we did and during the writing process itself, assisting each other in keeping to deadlines (for the most part). Fred influenced Meghan to get on board with the initial idea submission and through the support he lent from previous writing experiences. Meghan was able to help Fred flesh out ideas and bring a different perspective to see the project through. As in any relationship, we both influence and are influenced as we work together.

Understanding influence and leverage is simply part of the equation. The other parts are recognizing the complexities of influence and leverage (we'll talk about that now) and seeing how we can use influence and leverage to continue the good work we're striving toward (we'll talk about that later).

What becomes more and more clear as we gain a deeper understanding of influence and leverage is that using them effectively is a delicate dance. They are fluid and as dependent on the environmental circumstances as the people involved. It's helpful to think of influence and leverage as being affected by three factors, which we'll call the three Rs. In any given situation, a person's role, resources, and respect level can all have an impact on whether influence can be used and whether leverage is a factor.

Role

The impact of role on influence has a long history. In his article in *Harvard Business Review*, leadership coach Nick Morgan (2015) puts it simply enough: "People with power over others tend to talk more, to interrupt more, and to guide the conversation more" (para. 2). Generally speaking, those with supervisory roles tend to have greater influence on the direction of a relationship and are much more likely to use leverage effectively. Of course, it's entirely possible (and quite common) for direct reports to influence their supervisors. However, that has less to do with the role and more to do with the other two factors—resources and respect—which we'll focus on shortly.

Role-based influence, often referred to as *positional power*, requires little work on the part of the holder to use. The fact that a person is in an influencing role is all that's needed. Although role-based influence happens everywhere, it doesn't always allow for the greatest leverage. It can easily be diluted, particularly if resources and respect are lacking. As an aside, role-based influence exists in our personal lives, too. Parents exert it over their children, and spousal or partner relationships often have one of the partners serving in a diminished role to the other (at least in some capacity). For instance, Fred tends to be a greater influencer in how finances are handled in the family, whereas his wife is the keeper of all things schedule-wise. The bottom line is that influence and leverage can't exist on the basis of role alone.

Resources

Another way in which we exert influence is through the allocation of resources. Although often tied to role-based influence, influence based on resources can be wholly separate. Sometimes items or ideas that others have are very valuable to us and can prompt us to change our practice in a variety of ways. Tangible resources might include reading an article, listening to a TED Talk, or getting more digital devices in your school. Other resources are less concrete. For example, you might tour a school and see a productive planning cycle and then be inspired to reallocate time, space, or substitutes to allow the same planning to happen in your school. Resource-based influence is tricky because it often reflects the impact of intrinsic and extrinsic motivation. At times, access to resources is enough to make the difference; at others, our internal selves seal the deal, and resources that others have are not enough to move us forward (or back). You might choose a new job based on opportunity, personal goals, or passion even if the salary is lower or the school doesn't have the level of technology you desire. Resources are balanced against our personal motivations. Whether that access is to a person as a fountain of ideas or to an opportunity to obtain the most recently purchased educational technology tools, our ability to "grab" and "trade" resources provides ample opportunity to leverage a relationship.

Respect

The third *R* is the most difficult to predict and regularly plays out as a wild card. Respect is enough to lead to influence regardless of role or resources; when paired with one (or both) of those two, it can make the influence so strong and can provide so much leverage that the person or people on the other side of the relationship truly feel compelled to change. The greatest part about influence through respect is that it requires little more than doing what's right and what hopefully is best for others. The hardest part? If we lose others' respect, it is incredibly difficult to restore.

Let's go back to the influence worksheet that we completed earlier in this chapter (see Figure 2.1, p. 25) and take a look at Part II, which asks us to consider a number of our current relationships and reflect on the roles, resources, and respect in play. When you look over these details, who wields the influence and leverage? Why or why not?

Networking and Influence

To incorporate leverage, a relationship must be present. Professional relationships are formed and bolstered initially through networking—the act of communicating for benefit. This benefit must be mutual to maintain and sustain a connection; otherwise, it remains a one-time networking experience. As we dive deeper into influence and leverage in this chapter, it would be helpful to review the three interdependent yet distinct forms of networking that we discussed in Chapter 1: operational, personal, and strategic (see Ibarra, 2006; Ibarra & Hunter, 2007).

Operational Networking

Operational networking is the must-do networking to accomplish a task or get a job done. In schools, this can be as broad as the entire staff working on all functions necessary to keep the school operational, or as small as a team of three teachers organizing fundraising efforts. The breadth of the network isn't what defines operational networking; instead, it's the function of the network itself.

Several education organizations are working together to host a statewide conference on equity in education. Owing to a previous contact, the math and Multi-Tiered Systems of Support (MTSS) departments of a number of schools are now fully supporting the planning and delivery of the conference. Meetings are taking place more frequently as the event approaches, and various individuals—including the director of secondary mathematics, the director of a statewide teacher

> fellowship, a local teacher specialist, a support staff member from the Department of Education, and a representative from a local curriculum development company sponsoring the event—are interacting to get the event off the ground. These relationships may or may not be valuable after the work is complete, but there's ample opportunity to network and form relationships among the organizations and individuals working on the event.

We see operational networking in action when organizations work together to create an event. Routine, short-term demands are a hallmark of operational networking and, as such, they're unlikely to yield the deep and meaningful leverage points we need when striving to make change. Although the relationships fostered might create important contacts for the future, individuals are all working to complete a task; once the task is complete, connections can falter and dissipate. Influence can be exerted here, but it often doesn't need to be because the work and responsibilities are typically clear and the roles and tasks are defined.

Personal Networking

Personal networking is the most popular definition of the term—that is, networking outside a social circle but within a professional context with the aim of advancing a career or position. Because it involves an intentional and strategic move to engage with people with common goals or careers, personal networking can be superficial and can be sustained by a common association, group, or club. Personal networks have the advantage of providing a safe environment for sharing and receiving feedback and advice, and people often draw on them to more effectively complete a task. Influence is regularly applied in these situations, particularly to find work and bolster connections.

> When Fred first moved into a regional science role, he wasn't sure how best to proceed. He had experience as a classroom teacher and department chair, but, as often happens in a school system, he was siloed to the wants and needs of the specific community he worked in. He began attending science teacher conferences that a science organization held and started to present at those conferences. He wrote articles for the journal that the organization publishes and connected with educators on social media. He also co-led a Twitter chat with a colleague he had recently met. He soon built connections with educators who worked for the science organization, a number of whom supported him in his new science role and who still play a role in his work today.

The potential of a personal network to become something stronger and longer lasting is high. Everyone is only six degrees of separation from Kevin Bacon, after all. That principle suggests that when we need something from our professional network, if the person we ask doesn't know, chances are he or she knows someone who does or who can provide the influence to help us figure it out. The struggle is to grow such a network in an organic way so connections are meaningful and can be relied on. Allen Blue (2016), LinkedIn cofounder, suggests only connecting with others if you're willing to do them a favor. This simple baseline ensures you develop the depth of relationship necessary for professional networks to be mutually beneficial, and it strongly supports the idea of relationships existing in a transactional way.

Strategic Networking

Otherwise known as "where the magic happens," strategic networking is the mythical magical network that creates connections, keeps you informed, and propels personal and career goals. Strategic networks enable individuals to see the broad landscape, connect with key players, and leverage relationships to make change. In fact, according to Ibarra and Hunter (2007), "The key to a good strategic network is leverage: the ability to marshal information, support, and resources from one sector of a network to achieve results in another" (p. 44).

Meghan attended a conference to present on behalf of an organization, and she didn't know too many people there. She saw someone she happened to know and struck up a conversation. It turned out they had several areas of professional interest in common, and they had many of the same connections and goals. Later in the week, this same friend introduced Meghan to key players in a national organization—one she ultimately took a fellowship with. Meghan was able to leverage one relationship to create another; in effect, she turned an organizational and a personal connection into a strategic network that propelled her career goals.

Is it luck? It seems the lucky get luckier. There's always the right place at the right time, but strategic networking is far more than that. You need to place yourself in the right circles (through personal networking) and start the process of building relationships (often with operational networking) that you can leverage for the greatest impact. This requires an understanding of what's important to you, what's important to others, and why those things are important to where you hope to go and to what you hope to achieve.

If we want to propel our connections from networking to full-fledged relationships, we must use the four keys we discussed in Chapter 1: listening, trust, respect, and collaboration. As operational and personal networks overlap and mesh to support strategic networking, you're laying the groundwork to form stronger and deeper relationships. With this understanding of the basics of networks and networking, we'll now dive deeper into influence and how to wield it.

A Short History of Influence

Before understanding how we can influence others, it's helpful to look at some of the theories of influence and see how we can take what we know from large-scale systems, such as television advertising, and pare it down to useful messaging in personal relationships.

Following World War II, as film, television, and radio industries were expanding rapidly, a theory about influence became popular. It stated that mass media has an immediate and powerful effect on those who are exposed to it. This "magic bullet" theory of persuasion supposes that the sender of information is powerful and that the receiver is passive, only making a choice that they're told to make.

It's easy to see why this theory was backed at a time when Hitler had monopolized mass media, persuasion through propaganda and television was popularized, and media didn't allow for interactivity.

Could the masses be so susceptible? A radio program that aired in 1938 is the hallmark example of the magic bullet theory. H. G. Wells's *War of the Worlds* was broadcast to approximately 12 million people across the United States. It's estimated that more than one million of those listeners truly believed that Grover Mill, New Jersey, was under alien invasion, resulting in traffic jams as people fled for safety.

Is this theory so nefarious? Although the example of Hitler appealing to the masses through control of media is certainly an egregious case of influence, other examples of influence use have benefited society. In the 1930s, Franklin Delano Roosevelt took to the airwaves to speak directly to the American people about a variety of topics, from banking to unemployment to fighting fascism in Europe. Many point to his radio campaign as proof that a golden voice on radio can sway the masses (Katz & Lazarsfeld, 1955). A study of his presidency shifted the theory of influence to what is known as the *two-step flow model*, which says that most people form their opinions under the influence of opinion leaders, who, in turn, are influenced by the mass media. Its relevance to leveraging influence today is undeniable. The magic bullet theory, which seemed so promising in the early days of widespread communication, was debunked.

Teacher leaders on the school community council hear from the principal about a new app being used at several local schools to track reading progress and comprehension. The teacher leaders conduct a good deal of research, looking at online reviews of the app and other supporting data. They consider their belief in the administrator as a level-headed decision maker with solid pedagogical knowledge and decide that this app should be in all classrooms in the school. These teacher leaders then chat with colleagues, share their knowledge with parents, and ultimately report back to the principal, who agrees the app should be used schoolwide. These several teachers became the opinion leaders who swayed the staff and community to their belief, illustrating the two-step flow model in action.

In 1947, the *spiral of silence theory* came into existence. Conceptualized as a way to explain how poor leaders were able to gain support when many people disagreed with their positions, this theory still holds true. The premise is simple: people stay silent when they feel they're in the minority (Noelle-Neumann, 1984). It's an exercise in self-preservation; people don't want to be viewed as an outsider or risk isolation from the larger group. Conversely, the closer people feel their view is to the general public opinion, the more likely they are to voice their thinking.

With the spiral of silence, people will withhold their views, especially when the prevailing view devalues the wide array of ideas that may make up those people's perspectives. When only the loudest group is willing to speak their minds, it becomes the majority opinion by default. By using the forces discussed later in this book, we can shift conversations to see all viewpoints. Creating a system where relationships can thrive based on listening, trust, respect, and collaboration will also support varying views.

A principal wanted to vote on extending the school day. Her reasoning was that the school's after-school tutoring programs could really benefit everyone and that if they just added time to the day, they could all provide more intervention in the classroom. One teacher didn't want to extend the day; she was already arriving by 7:00 in the morning, and she worked until 4:00 or 5:00 in the afternoon. She didn't even get a break during lunch or recess; she had duties to carry out during both. Three or four people spoke up fervently in favor of the extended day, so the teacher felt pressured to vote for it. The following year, as burnout was at an all-time high, there was more and more grumbling in the halls. Teachers were collectively spent. It turns out that most people didn't want to vote for extending the day at all, but they felt they had to do so because of the principal and the few loud speakers who were in favor of the move. How things might have shifted had those teachers not been afraid to speak up!

Influence in the modern era has evolved as our media has become more plentiful and interactive. We're more likely than ever to use media as entertainment or an escape. Ownership and control of media experiences are firmly in the hands of the user, which is completely opposite to the magic bullet theory.

Perhaps simplistic to a fault, the *uses and gratifications theory* says that we seek out media to be gratified or because we have a particular use for the object. Consider cell phones. They're designed for a use (contacting friends and family), but they also gratify us in a variety of ways (Leung & Wei, 2000). We use our phones and the services they provide for entertainment, to shop, and to self-gratify with likes and retweets.

If we're talking about human gratification, it's because we can exponentially strengthen our networks when we meet others' needs in these areas. According to Katz and Blumler (1974), human gratification is divided into five categories:

- **Affective needs.** The emotional gratification we feel from watching a movie or reading a book in which we identify with the characters is an affective need. We seek these outlets for entertainment value, but we also seek to connect emotionally with the experience.

- **Cognitive needs.** We need outlets that support cognition. When we seek out articles, news sources, or reviews that provide us with insight into how things work, we're supporting our cognitive needs.

- **Social integrative needs.** Our human need to feel connected to others drives a social integrative need. This is what makes us seek out ways to connect through Twitter, Facebook, and Instagram. Mass media can also serve as the springboard to post thoughts online and engage in discussion on media platforms.

- **Personal integrative needs.** Self-esteem and respect are driving forces for personal integrative needs. It's not only about garnering likes or followers. Media can also identify what styles are popular or what brands we should use to gain the respect of others. People may mimic traits they see in characters in order to be seen as having those traits themselves.

- **Tension-free needs.** Research suggests that teaching is the second most stressful job after ambulance driving, so it's no wonder that escaping through media is a highly sought-out pastime (Johnson et al., 2005). Tension-free needs indicate a desire to move out of our regular lives for a short time, with the result that we feel more recharged when we return to work.

When we provide information, support, and solutions that meet these needs for others, we not only strengthen our networks but also create a situation in which those we seek to influence are highly receptive.

Using Influence and Leverage Effectively

Understanding that influence and leverage are key parts of our interactions with others and that they're good things when used well, it's worth exploring a number of strategies that make the best use of them.

Know Your Audience

One key aspect of our work is making sure we know *who* we'll be influencing and *how* we'll be applying leverage. Some people respond better than others to being influenced; some actually prefer to be influenced to accomplish their work. Knowing who needs and welcomes being influenced—and knowing who doesn't—can be the difference between a relationship that continues to grow and one that's constantly wilting. If you haven't seen the famous TED Talk on starting a movement by Derek Sivers (2010), it's worth a view to understand the implications of knowing who people are, how they operate, and what they need (there's a link to the TED Talk in the References section of this book). How can you tell if others are open to influence? Here are three ways:

1. The person regularly solicits your input, particularly around high-stakes decisions.
2. The person is a born questioner and is just as comfortable asking questions as having the answers (these people often find themselves in the Wonderer role we mentioned in Chapter 1).
3. The person is comfortable acting on the ideas of others, as opposed to acting solely on his or her own ideas.

When we consider another person's openness to influence, we're more likely to use it at the right time and in the right way.

Fred had begun to recognize that the same approaches to getting work done wouldn't necessarily work with different people. When some of his early leadership requests ended less favorably than he might have hoped, he started to realize, thanks to excellent coaching and support from supervisors and mentors, that he needed to make some shifts. He started letting those he was engaged in conversation with express their needs and wants *before* he made any requests. He started incorporating a number of strategies, including paraphrasing and focusing on actions, rather than on people or their personality traits, to better balance out the direction of the discussion for anyone involved. Most important, he made sure to really get to know people's interests and needs before applying any influence, something that worked well for him in the classroom and that has worked equally as well in his current role as director of curriculum and instruction.

Do No Harm

A crucial point we make in this book is that our use of influence should never be exercised with the intention to harm. Rather, we should set our sights on outcomes that benefit those with whom we interact, as well as all those who are affected by our decisions. Doing no harm when it comes to using influence and leverage is pretty easy. It simply requires us to ask ourselves two key questions:

- Are my intentions for using influence or leverage in this situation for the greater good?
- If I were to look back on this relationship interaction, would I feel better or worse for having used influence and leverage?

If we can answer both of these questions in a way that feels good, we should be comfortable putting influence and leverage into practice.

Apply Freely and Know When to Stop

Like moisturizer, influence and leverage can and should be applied liberally, assuming that you know your audience and that your use of influence and leverage won't intentionally do any harm. That said, you shouldn't overuse these tools. Consider your favorite meal. If you could, you might eat it regularly and often. But every day? Chances are, you'd get sick of it faster than you can say "influence and leverage." So it pays for us to keep tabs on how we've used these influence and leverage tools and with whom. If we use them too often or, for that matter, too infrequently, we're missing the point of influence and leveraging decision making.

With a deeper understanding of influence and leverage, we can now shift our focus in the next chapter to exploring the four ways we can help others continue to do good work.

Questions for Self-Reflection
- What are some of the ways you've used influence in your current role? How have others influenced you?
- In what ways might you help others see the value in a supply-and-demand relationship view?

Questions for Group Discussion
- What lessons can we learn from the history of influence? How does our current landscape shift the needle on the use of influence and leverage?
- How can we prevent others from taking a negative perspective of this view?

3

The Forces of Influence

The term *relationship* generally brings to mind friendship, collegiality, and closeness, when truly, relationships can be between acquaintances or between employer and employee. How and why relationships form at varying degrees of intensity have a lot to do with the type of need driving the relationship. Humans are social creatures, so relationships are necessary. We tend to enjoy the company of others, and this is why relationships often have a romantic or familial feel.

There are other reasons relationships form. Decision making can be more effective if we consider various viewpoints. Successful organizations model this thinking with executive boards, leadership teams, and committees. Hearing from all sides on an issue helps ward off unexpected opposition after decisions are made and can lend a supportive team culture to any situation. Sometimes we enjoy working with those of a similar mind, but relationships regularly blossom among opposites. Take the case of working on a school grade-level team. The team works in the same system and school and teaches the same content, but each team member brings different strengths and varied experience to the group.

Perhaps most important, relationships form from needs and wants. Now, to suggest that we all want something from every relationship feels a little sleazy. We're quick to say, "No, I only want to give here." The reality is, every relationship, no matter how successful or dysfunctional, forms from a base level of needs or wants. The five categories of human gratification that we discussed in Chapter 2 also come into play as relationships form.

Social integrative needs might be considered the catchall for relationships. There's a human desire to connect to others at any level. All relationships are formed off this basic need to connect. *Affective needs* drive our emotional desire to be with others. Friends at work make us more comfortable in the work environment; coworkers who will help shoulder responsibility help us relax; and broader acceptance by the group makes us feel better, more productive, and happier. *Cognitive needs* drive relationships based on learning. Connecting with a professional learning network or even engaging in heated discussion around pressing topics helps serve our cognitive needs. We tend to build relationships that give us safe spaces to stretch our thinking and help us develop personally and professionally.

Personal integrative needs drive our desire for acceptance, respect, and self-esteem. Someone might form relationships through a professional organization with the end goal of appearing more competent and connected in his or her field. The deep-seated human desire to like ourselves and have others regard us positively can be the foundation for many relationships. Finally, *tension-free needs* push us to create relationships that help us escape the normal day-to-day demands of life, even if in a small way. This doesn't mean that all tension-free needs are completely outside work; they may just require us to change the context. Relationships with teachers from other schools might serve this purpose, as well as personal relationships unrelated to our careers.

The Forces of Influence Leadership Matrix

There's a continuum of relationship building, and knowing how and why relationships exist lays a foundation for understanding how we function in each one we form. The way you influence your team might differ from how you interact with your administrator. To see where you tend to operate, consider the Forces of Influence Leadership Matrix (FILM) shown in Figure 3.1.

First, think about several different instances when you've tried to influence others in your school, district, or organization. You might consider interactions with coworkers, teams, administrators, parents, students, and support staff. On the matrix, mark your position on the horizontal continuum by considering how involved you like to be on the front end of influencing others. If you're on the extreme left-hand side, for instance, you enjoy putting minimal effort into getting things started. You like to toss out ideas without delving into the history of a topic or taking the time for context. You're more likely to act on impulse than plan for every contingency. You prefer to jump right in and get rockin' and rollin'. Conversely, if you're on the far right side, you likely prefer acting as the tortoise rather than the hare. You like to carefully plan and think through every possibility before getting started. You'll come to meetings having thoroughly researched the history of the decision or topic under review. You like to know all the data and be able to justify decisions before

Figure 3.1 **Forces of Influence Leadership Matrix**

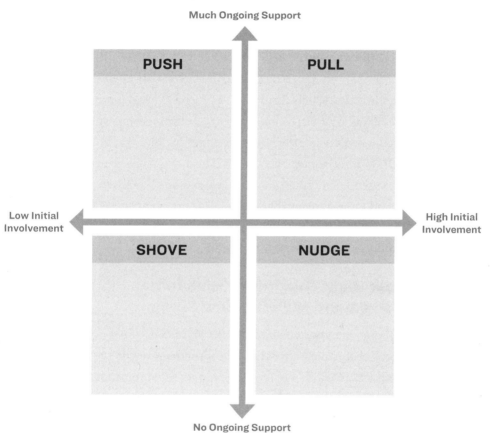

even engaging in a conversation. Considering these extremes, put a mark on the horizontal continuum to indicate where you tend to fall when influencing others.

Next, consider the vertical continuum. Mark your position on this line by considering how involved you like to be after a decision has been made. If you fall at the bottom of the line, you generally don't provide ongoing support, which is not as disparaging as it might sound. When decisions are made, you want them to be carried out. You tend to disseminate and delegate tasks to other people. On the extreme upper part of the line, you want to see the entire process through to the end. You're likely to take on tasks yourself, walk through an experience hand-in-hand with a colleague, and generally be intricately involved in a process throughout its lifetime. Considering your usual commitment to ongoing support of an idea or a task, mark where you fall on the vertical line.

Draw a horizontal line and a vertical line from the two points you located to find their intersection, and you'll see what quadrant you tend to operate in when influencing others to take action. Now that you know where you commonly fall on the matrix, let's assign some values to each of these quadrants.

Upper Right Quadrant = High Initial Involvement, High Ongoing Support

If you find yourself in the upper right box, you're involved in decisions before and after they occur. You tend to put a lot of background and research into anything you do, and "preparation" is your middle name. You may find yourself taxed because you teeter into overcommitment and are unlikely to delegate work to others, but you also have a great capacity for building relationships because you put in the time and ongoing support required to keep relationships moving forward. A person in this category is no stranger to shouldering responsibility and probably enjoys diving deep into topics.

Upper Left Quadrant = Low Initial Involvement, High Ongoing Support

In this quadrant, requests are often immediate. You usually need fast results and appreciate a quick dive into decision making.

Operating in this quadrant requires little or no preparation on your part. If you're working in this part of the matrix, you may enjoy brainstorming, getting all the ideas out on the table, and getting a quick response to each course of action proposed. People in this quadrant do feel an obligation to support ideas for the long haul. As long as you get started, you're willing to jump right in and help. The downside here is that you might become a micromanager or take too much on your plate because you feel the obligation to keep things moving. You might not consider all viable solutions, and you might run the risk of generating compliance rather than exercising true influence.

Lower Left Quadrant = Low Initial Involvement, Low Ongoing Support

A person operating in this quadrant makes immediate suggestions to and requests of others. This quadrant requires little or no preparation to drive influence. If you operate in this quadrant, you would, as in the upper left box, enjoy brainstorming and quick-moving decisions. The difference here is that operating in this quadrant doesn't feel like an ongoing obligation to support ideas. Instead, a person in this segment of the matrix delegates responsibility or relies on others to complete tasks. This isn't necessarily negative; some people work best when they're not managed too closely. A person operating in this quadrant demands results; a request made here might feel more like a command. This box often breeds compliance. When overused, it's unlikely to promote deep relationship building.

Lower Right Quadrant = High Initial Involvement, Low Ongoing Support

The final quadrant comprises people who like to thoroughly think through all options and research the background on any decision. They're ready to pull out facts, figures, and supporting documents at a moment's notice because they read them all before making a suggestion. People in this quadrant like to do the work on the front end; they enjoy the setup, the decision making, and the research. This part of the matrix doesn't usually entail ongoing support, however. Once a decision is made, people in this quadrant feel OK letting the work play out without their involvement. Influence here can be overlooked because of the subtlety of the actions taken. And although there's little likelihood of the people in this quadrant being called micromanagers, influences in play here might be overlooked altogether.

The Forces: An Overview

So now that we have a sense of the areas we tend to focus on and the regions of the matrix where most of our roles and relationships tend to live, it makes sense to explore each of the quadrants to set context and pave the way for the rest of this book.

The Pull

Pulls are incredibly special forces. As you can see from the Forces of Influence Leadership Matrix that you just completed, a pull is separate from all the other quadrants in that it requires high levels of initial investment in a relationship interaction, as well as sustained work and support throughout that experience. This means that as a "puller," you're invested in the situation throughout. For better or worse. Until the end of the situation do you part. In pulls, all those involved play a pivotal role. This type of interaction leaves no one out and provides no shade for an involved relationship member to hide under. All parties are exposed, and all are expected to help the situation reach a positive ending. In this type of situation, it's one for all and all for one; the person initiating the pull and those being pulled either bring the situation to a fruitful conclusion or, as the unfortunately named group The Chainsmokers writes in their chart-topping song "Paris," "We all go down together." Pulls could be you and a colleague creating and presenting a session during a district-based conference day or you and your grade-level teachers designing a new math unit of study. Because a lot of energy and resources are put into this type of influence move, those wishing to use it need to plan carefully at the start and throughout to have as productive an experience as possible. Pulls can be very rewarding, but they're also often incredibly tiring for all involved.

The Push

A push gets others to take the next step. This often means not just encouraging others to grow but also requiring them to do so. Although the push tends to require most of the initial work to be on the part of the pushee, the person initiating the push is always waiting just offstage to provide support, counseling, and mentoring as the performer being pushed grows in his or her practice. Although a push can be initiated relatively easily, it necessitates a well-orchestrated plan throughout on the part of the person initiating the push to ensure that those being pushed feel supported and cared for throughout the learning experience. In many situations, mentor/mentee relationships exist throughout a series of long-term pushes. Student teaching, when done right, is often one extended push, helping the student teacher to grow in his or her practice and the mentor to support others.

The Shove

Like the other three forces, the shove is not appropriate in every situation. A shove is an influence move where we refrain from providing much investment at all. This can be very difficult or very easy; it all depends on why we're shoving someone and how he or she will respond. By investing little in the initiation of the force and by refraining from providing support throughout the experience, we're essentially leaving the results of the situation up to others. In this method of leveraging relationships, we're not simply taking the monkey off our back—we're forcing it to stay on someone else's. A principal might delegate responsibility to a grade-level chair without providing a lot of background or support, assuming the work will be done in a timely manner because the grade-level chair has been given a directive. A superintendent might share elements of a strategic plan with district and building leaders without diving into details or assisting with implementation. This method of influencing others is often seen as a make-or-break moment; all involved can come out of the situation either empowered and stronger than before, or utterly defeated. When we employ this strategy, we apply the most extreme force. By its nature, a single shove can drastically change relationships.

The Nudge

We've all been nudged by others, and likely have used the nudge with some degree of success in the past. This force's value is also tied to its difficulty of use. Successful nudging requires intense preplanning. It isn't enough to know the people we hope to nudge; rather, we have to be so in tune with their needs that our involvement seems almost invisible. Why? Because to craft a meaningful nudge, we need to lay the groundwork and then get out of the way. In nudges that bring about change, the nudgee might have no idea that he or she has been influenced by someone else. We've all been nudged by others and, likely, we didn't even know it. When this strategy is well designed and well intentioned, it can lead others to grow and feel stronger about themselves as learners and leaders.

Because those being nudged tend to come to their own conclusions, this force can sometimes be the only type of leverage we can apply in positional power situations where we're the ones without the position or power. For example, a teacher who wants to implement an arts-based science program might distribute supporting articles to gain traction with other teachers and the administration. A colleague might share the writing she has done for a professional organization, trying to convince others to do the same. This has tremendous value because it can enable us to help others, regardless of their position, to make positive change and revise their thinking (with a little help from us) to benefit learners.

With all the forces now defined, take a look back at the quadrant where you tend to live most frequently. Can you relate to your dominant force? Do your practices of learning and leading seem to mesh with how that force operates? What quadrant do you tend to live in least? What does that mean for your work moving forward?

To pave the way for the next series of chapters, we're going to conduct a self-assessment before moving forward (see Figure 3.2). The Roles and Relationships Self-Assessment will help you think about the roles and actions we take and the force that most likely aligns with that action. This self-assessment is useful to determine whether the quadrant we believe we live in is supported by the actions we take. For now, complete Part I of the self-assessment. After we explore each of the forces in more depth in Chapters 4–7, we'll ask you to refer back to Part II and add more detail to your self-assessment.

With that in mind, we'll now "pull" ourselves (and all of you) along to the next chapter!

Figure 3.2 Roles and Relationships Self-Assessment

This tool will help you look at the roles you take on and the relationships you engage in to give you a deeper understanding of the methods you use to lead and learn.

Part I: Complete the first two columns of the chart below by including the roles you take on during a normal day and the actions you take in those roles. What commonalities do you see? Do your actions differ on the basis of a given role?

Part II: Complete this part of the tool after reading Chapters 4–7, which tackle each of the four Forces of Influence (pull, push, shove, nudge). In the third column, list the forces used for each of the actions you noted in Part I.

Role	Actions Taken in That Role	Force of Influence Used

Questions for Self-Reflection

- The boxes of the quadrant represent the intensity that exists across forces. How might a pull be more or less intense? What does intensity look like in a given force?
- Being initially involved in a situation and providing continued support require different skills. What do you see as necessary for each of these force ingredients? What do you tend to view as a strength? As a struggle?

Questions for Group Discussion

- What are some of the key similarities and differences we see among the forces across the matrix?
- What are the implications of the forces for the work we do as a school or district community?

The Pull

If you're reading this text sequentially, you'll notice that the next four chapters dive into each of the four Forces of Influence in more detail. We've decided to structure this deep dive by emphasizing the what, when, why, and how for pulls, pushes, shoves, and nudges. You'll learn more about what they are, when to use them, why you would want to use them, and how to put them into practice. In addition, you'll see that we've sprinkled in tools you can use to build your influence toolkit, as well as multiple ways to use the Forces of Influence Leadership Matrix as a foundation for your work.

And if you aren't reading this sequentially? Then don't worry, you probably haven't come across this paragraph yet.

> Changing teaching positions is always tough, but entering an environment that doesn't support what you know to be best practices can be particularly difficult. Meghan entered a new school, taking on a supposedly better and more desirable teaching position, with high hopes for the teaching utopia

she had been promised. What she found were incredible educators who, for a variety of reasons, were not equipped to employ best practices. Having spent years in a system that developed certain skills, such as close reading, Meghan wanted to share the impact that such practices could have on student achievement. After all, if the students in her previous position, many of whom were facing adversity, could attain success, why couldn't these seemingly more privileged students do the same?

Unfortunately, no one was willing to dive in; fear of failure, lack of time, and pressure to show student growth kept everyone from dipping their toes in the water. Meghan wasn't OK with this disregard for successful practices, or with shutting her door when she knew what was right. Somehow she needed to get everyone on board, yet she was just a new coworker with no real authority to demand change.

Meghan selected one skill, in this case close reading, that aligned with a school and district goal at the time: get every child engaged in critical reading. She shared her resources, which she'd collected over years of training and implementation, with the reading coach and sat down with her to answer questions about the process. Meghan partnered with one of the 9th grade teachers and volunteered to coteach classes. The teacher would come visit Meghan's class and watch her teach close reading, then the two would coteach their classes. Finally, Meghan watched her colleague teach both classes. The two shifted schedules and students around to be able to work together. Once the colleague felt comfortable and confident, both of them started sharing feedback during the weekly grade-level meetings and sharing work with the reading coach. Not only did students become better readers and writers, but the teaching culture also shifted to reflect a growing openness of practice and support to help all kids.

The What

Have you ever been near the dance floor, enjoying the music, but not feeling particularly interested in jumping into the scene? You want to maintain the illusion of cool, and what better way to ruin that than to dance and flail in front of the crowd? Then an overzealous friend grabs your arm, pulls you onto the dance floor, and provides a safety net. Your friend dances along with you, and all of a sudden, you're a dancing fool. This is a pull—a strategically placed friend who provides the kickstart (in the form of sick dance moves you can mimic) and the ongoing support (laughing along with you as you both make fools of yourselves) to make a change.

One advantage of the pull is that it relies on the research-based elements of coaching models. Pulls work particularly well when one person doesn't have management over another, which is great when you want to influence change from a non-administrative position. The kind of trusting relationship that can be formed during a pull is a key component of effective coaching (Burley & Pomphrey, 2011). Trust is a necessary part of relationship building, and relationships form the basis of influence. As Marzano, Simms, Roy, Heflebower, and Warrick (2013) note, "Strong relationships . . . develop organizational trust within a school and help school members understand that they can turn to one another for help and support" (pp. 9–10).

Pulls require high initial involvement. This is reflected in many different ways. You might search for information and become the thought leader in a given situation. You might have extensive personal experience that supports your position. You might spend time simply discussing ideas with others and gathering their feedback. Before you're ready to influence others, you have to bring a certain level of commitment to the process.

That said, you don't have to be an expert when using this influence strategy. Because you'll be providing ongoing support, you can learn alongside the person you're pulling. Leading by example is fine, but leading by doing the hard work collaboratively can be more effective. And it isn't just in the world of education. A study appearing in the *Harvard Business Review* (Ibarra & Hansen, 2011) found that the top chief executive officers in the world play the role of connector and model collaboration. They also "engage talent in the periphery" (p. 71). In other words, they grab those standing at the edge of the dance floor and pull them in.

The When

A pull is certainly an all-in proposition. This force becomes imperative when you need to drive change but when you also have the time and ability to foster a relationship. As we will explore in Chapter 6, shoves operate with a critical timeline; change is needed, and it must happen now. By contrast, a pull can take time to develop and put into motion. And unlike nudges, pulls inherently imply an ongoing support structure; the person using this strategy has to commit for the long haul.

Consider a data dive. When it's implemented with best practices, teachers, coaches, and administrators come together with some background and knowledge. A coach will have looked at trends in data, as well as at past and upcoming assessments, and will know the history of the students involved while bringing a variety of skills, tips, tricks, and resources to the table. And although such an initiative likely arose from the administrative or coaching side, those pullers will continue to work alongside teachers to shift practice. Coauthoring, copresenting, and coteaching are all vivid instances of the power of pulling.

Here's when this influence tool is most useful:

- **When relationships are valued.** By their nature, pulls rely on some previous context. Pulls usually happen when there's an existing relationship between the puller and pullee. In the case of new relationships, pulls can actually foster relationship building by being a value-added and ongoing partnership. Personal affective needs and cognitive needs can both be met through the use of this strategy. Alternatively, when a relationship exists or even needs repair, a pull can foster shared responsibility and trust because the person enacting the pull is working alongside the one being pulled. The deeper the existing relationship, the more quickly a pull is likely to have an impact.

- **When hierarchy doesn't matter, or maybe when it really matters.** Pulls balance relationships, because the initiator has to work closely with the pullee. When the person who is applying the influence is in an administrative position, that person shows his or her willingness to do the day-to-day work, garnering trust among those being influenced. When the puller is in a subordinate position, it levels the playing field. The puller serves as a team player able and willing to put forth new ideas, be an expert, and work to drive change. Pulls can be even more powerful when the hierarchical structure is totally removed; coworkers, friends, and equals are often the most powerful influencers of their peers.

- **When time isn't a factor.** Certainly there's a need to change when any type of force comes into play, but some changes occur faster than others. The subtlety of a nudge can take time, whereas a shove can move change quickly. A pull needs time to make real change. True, bringing a friend to the dance floor is an instantaneous decision, but it's built on a previous relationship. When developing a relationship or working on a particularly precarious idea, it takes time to build trust. It also takes time (and effort) to stay involved for the long haul. If you can't dedicate the time, a pull isn't going to work.

Consider the following positive and negative qualities of the pull. Note that pulls aren't inherently either positive or negative; rather, they're based entirely on the situation. Situational context has to be considered when contemplating the consequences of any force.

- **The positives:**
  - Pulls are obvious; they're transparent because you're working alongside the person you wish to influence and making your position known.
  - Titles, positions, and power don't matter. Anyone can pull on someone, regardless of status.
  - Pulls require strategic planning, an important skill to build and use in influencing others across contexts.
  - The shared responsibility and work inherent in pulls are a rising tide that lifts all ships. Pullers get what they want from the situation while building capacity in others.

- **The negatives:**
  - Because pulls are obvious, any retribution or blowback is assigned to the puller.
  - A lack of positional power means that actions are mandated. Pullers have to be OK with the possibility that their pull is ignored.
  - It's work! A pull requires high involvement in planning, researching, and overseeing the initiative.
  - As with most forces, pulls can strain relationships. This is especially true when the pullee resists change and feels put upon by the change.
  - Even though the puller has to provide ongoing support and involvement, gratitude might not ensue. When things go wrong, the puller can be blamed, but when things go right, the pullee alone may reap the rewards.

A Voice from the Field

As a high school administrator, I planned to evaluate one of my special education math teachers during a scheduled fall observation. To my surprise, the instructional assistant assigned to this class was at the whiteboard leading the class through a math problem. I was impressed by the assistant's natural talent and wondered whether she had ever been encouraged by administration to take the necessary steps to become licensed as a teacher. I brought this up with her after class was dismissed.

She laughed at my suggestion and said that no one had ever approached her in her 14 years of being an instructional assistant about becoming a teacher, and that she wasn't even sure how to become licensed. I explained the process to her, noting that the provisional license was temporary and that she would need to take additional classes and meet specific certifications to apply for the full teaching license. I let her know that the process might seem overwhelming, but that I would be there to support her every step of the way and that we would take it one step at a time.

Soon after, I received an e-mail from our licensing specialist regarding a local summer teaching program that would help individuals gain their provisional teaching license. I encouraged the instructional assistant to apply, submitting a letter of recommendation for her as well as proofreading her essays. She was accepted into the program and issued a provisional special education license that summer—and later on our school hired her to fill a full-time special education teacher position. After she was hired, I informed her that we would be meeting once every two weeks to discuss her progress not only as a special education teacher, but also as a full-time student in her education classes. I invited her to bring questions about assignments that did not quite make sense or come ready to discuss aha moments when she found connections between a theory she was learning in her coursework and its application to what she was seeing and implementing in the classroom. In time, and with my support, she grew into a highly talented classroom teacher.

I pulled my instructional assistant toward becoming a teacher because I knew not only that she had potential, but also, ultimately, that it would benefit my special education students who often struggle in math. Now that I'm an administrator, I can pay forward the gift of influence that was given to me time and time again as I journeyed forward in my own educational career. When influencing students or teachers, I call on the trusting relationships we have established to set the foundation for our work. Influencing others is like planting seeds; with time and attention, they and others will reap a harvest from their own hard work and dedication.

—Basil Marin
Assistant Principal, Churchland High School
Portsmouth, VA

If Assistant Principal Marin's pull hadn't worked, he would have missed out on a chance to capitalize on growing an incredible teacher in the school, and she might have missed out on her new career path. Regardless of the outcome, in this case a satisfying one, the instructional assistant felt valued and noticed, which only further builds relationships. And although there might come a day when Marin has to use a different type of force when interacting with this teacher, he's gone a long way to building a relationship through a well-placed, well-executed pull. Of course, just like in the cult movie classic *Clue*, the ending could have been totally different.

Marin could have lacked background as a respected leader, and then his pull wouldn't have carried as much weight. He could have lacked follow-through, and the assistant might not have progressed past accepting a great compliment. Why does a pull work so well in certain situations? Let's explore.

The Why

Take another look at the Forces of Influence Leadership Matrix that we discussed in Chapter 3 (see Figure 3.1, p. 45). One thing we notice right away about the pull is that it requires substantial amounts of work. With its high initial investment and the need for support and follow-up throughout the interaction, we can better understand why this method of influence demands so much input from all involved.

The high-energy approach of a pull helps to dictate why we need it. There are often elements of our work that are so large and all-encompassing that they can't be completed unless there is full oversight and involvement throughout. Another key reason why we need to focus on this strategy? At times, it isn't just about the scope of an experience; it can also be about knowing that others can change themselves—but only if we change ourselves alongside them. Let's take a look at these two categories in further detail.

The Big Pull

When we take the 36,000-foot view of education, it can be daunting to look around us. Change in education is particularly slow, owing partly to the fact that learning is multifaceted and messy. It isn't uncommon to become so uncomfortable with the slow pace of change that we assume that focusing on more will make us more efficient. And yet we all know this is problematic. Jim Collins, a leader in company sustainability and growth, notes, "The real path to greatness, it turns out, requires simplicity and diligence. . . . It demands each of us to focus on what is vital—and to eliminate all of the extraneous distractions" (Schmoker, 2016, p. 11).

The need for a laserlike focus on a few key goals speaks to the necessity of including pulls in our work. Because this is such an intensive force, if we want to use it effectively, we need to make sure that we're only pulling a few things at a time. A good rule of thumb is to consider the "two hands rule." It's simple: with two hands, it's only possible to pull two different things. To input the energy and oversight this strategy needs, we should engage in no more than two pulls at a time. Knowing that pulls work for big-ticket items that we anticipate will take a lot of energy and time to move to the finish line, it can be helpful to reflect on our focus before applying influence.

Once in a while, we need to step back and look at a program or service to determine how to make it valuable to the people it serves. A few years ago, Fred and a number of colleagues had to take that big-picture view of the environmental education program provided by their agency and shared with districts in their region. Changes needed to be made for schools and districts to use it fully, including redesigning lessons and programs to align with new science standards and working out an evolved pricing formula. As a large team,

Fred and his colleagues met to talk about what the program was and wasn't doing and identified outcomes that had been gathered from students, teachers, and leaders who were and weren't using the program. Once a direction was determined, it became apparent that the work would require an "all hands on deck" approach throughout; there was a lot of work to do that incorporated a larger skill set than any one person had. Fred and his supervisor at the time pulled each other (and a number of other staff members) to help restructure the program from top to bottom: new lessons, new staff, a new location, and new policies and procedures all came together, along with a renewed focus to bring the program in line with district needs. This allowed membership in the program to grow and the service to improve. Because of full buy-in from the whole team, the program feels more in tune with the region's mission, vision, and methods of innovating and partnering.

Hand-Holding

Supporting others by actively guiding them to reach a conclusion is as important a part of our work as is shooting for the moon and hoping to reach it. Although the community at large may not feel the effect of a pull, using a pull to support an individual (or individuals) can result in an impact on a small subset of the community that is literally off the charts.

It can feel nearly impossible to change an entire district, school, or even grade level, but by working alongside those individuals ready and willing to change, there's a greater chance of success. In Meghan's coaching position, coaches complete this work daily. During the first year of implementing a new mathematics program districtwide, coaches offered a monthly grade-level cohort meeting to teachers who were interested in learning more about the program and who wanted to be guided through implementation throughout the year. Coaches spent time anticipating misconceptions and teacher needs to plan effective professional learning. Teachers met monthly, discussed opportunities for improvement and successes, and received individualized attention throughout the year. Did this shift the entire systemwide implementation? No, but it had a huge effect in the way it enabled cohort members to reflect on their own practice, adopt unique models, plan and deliver lessons effectively, and embrace a growth mindset throughout the year.

Investing so much time and energy in helping a small group of others grow their practice speaks volumes. It also highlights why pulls require so much forethought in their use. How can we determine who is pull-worthy and who isn't? It's based on the situation at hand. To help identify potential pullees, we've created a short four-question tool (see Figure 4.1) that you can use before taking the step of planning your pull. This Pull Potential tool should only be used with those who seem to have the potential to help

Figure 4.1 **Pull Potential**

Use this tool to determine how likely a pull is to result in a large-scale return. Although it won't work in every situation, it will provide some context before you take the next step and plan your pull. Just as important, it will help you focus on the person or people you're working with and why.

Answer the following questions, record your answers, and add up the points. The number of points will give you a sense of whether a pull is warranted or whether a different force might be a better option.

1. When I consider the person I wish to pull, I identify that person's personality type as
   A. Slow and steady.
   B. Worrywart.
   C. Risk taker.
   D. Immovable object.

2. When I consider the timeline for this pull, it most likely could last
   A. One month.
   B. One year.
   C. One week.
   D. One day.

3. When I consider the person I wish to pull, I see that person's future with the organization as
   A. Being in it for the long haul.
   B. A stepping-stone to something else.
   C. Here today, gone tomorrow.
   D. In the words of the Magic 8 Ball, "Reply hazy, try again."

4. In considering pulling this person, I identify my interest in this work as
   A. Ready and willing.
   B. Needs to happen.
   C. Not feeling it.
   D. "Time. There's never any time!" (bonus points if you can identify this quote)

Award yourself 4 points for every "A," 3 points for every "B," 2 points for every "C," and 1 point for every "D." Add up the points and see how your tally aligns (or not) with the use of a pull.

- *14–16 points.* Pull! The person involved seems willing to do the work (and so are you). The timeline and your sense of the person's potential with your organization blend well with the time and effort you're willing to put into the use of this force.

- *11–13 points.* Although a pull makes sense here, there are some concerns for you to be aware of. Maybe you're already pulled in too many directions, or maybe the nature of the person is such that a pull will require more work than you anticipated. Regardless, a pull may still be the best choice, as long as you realize that there may be a bit of a tug-of-war along the way.

- *8–10 points.* Proceed with caution. You could use a pull, but it might come with significant risk. You might choose to pull in this scenario if no other force seems to fit. More likely, though, there are better options to help you accomplish your goal and benefit the person involved.

- *4–7 points.* Turn around, and do not pass go. A pull in this situation is a mismatch. You'll most likely be wasting your time and effort in a situation that would be better served by a different force. Reconsider your approach before moving forward.

the organization grow in the long term. We need to make sure our investment of time and energy will lead to more than simply us doing the work.

The How

Engaging in a pull can take some work. Going into it with anything other than 100 percent puts us at a significant disadvantage. With that in mind, here are some recommendations for how to best put a pull into practice.

Gauge Energy

One of the keys to "pulling off" a successful pull is determining how much energy potential pull partners have to put into the work. This isn't easy, but there are a number of look-fors to guide you in making this determination. Reflecting on the following questions can help:

- What do the people's days look like? Are they currently running from one opportunity (or fire) to the next? Do they have flex-time in their schedules to sit and reflect for a moment (or three)?
- How do they fare in the "coffee cup" test? (The test is simple; you gauge how much time people are away from their desks or classrooms when they go for coffee; the more time they have to do this, the more time and energy they'll likely have for a pull.) Are they chatting during their coffee run? What does their conversation sound like? Is it engaged? Just a passing hello?
- What does their practice look like? Do they start work strong and then sputter out? Do they tend to carry teams through to completion? Do they slowly get going?

- What is their level of energy when they come to their school or office? Are they generally higher energy and excitable or lower energy and calm?
- How invested in the potential work are they? Do they share your view on the importance of what you have planned? How much convincing will be necessary? (With a pull, too much convincing is a bad thing!)

We can also turn these questions inward to see if we're likely to be successful pullers. For instance, it's a good idea to run the coffee cup test on ourselves. Do *we* have the time to invest in a pull at this moment? How engaged can we be in the work of using this force?

Generally speaking, those whom we gauge to have the highest energy levels are also those who are most likely to be the best recipients of a pull. Lower-energy colleagues or colleagues who seem to have little time to reflect or chat (because they're overscheduled, for example) will struggle more with the time needed to put this strategy into practice. As with any of the forces, it's always better to know that a force is well matched going into a scenario. If you discover that it's not, you'll need to try to back out of it when a move doesn't work out (we'll explore this more in a later chapter).

Schedule Your Pull

As with any force that requires a significant amount of setup, scheduling your pull can be the difference between a rousing success and an unmitigated disaster. (Or we could say "dramatic," but who doesn't love using "unmitigated" in a sentence?) That's why we've designed the Pull Planner (see Figure 4.2). Like any strategic planning tool, the Pull Planner will enable you to think before you

Figure 4.2 **Pull Planner**

Challenge: The problem or challenge you want to solve
Desired Change: The resolution you desire
Impact (if/then): Your desired change written out as an if/then statement. For example, "*If* we do XYZ, *then* ___will be the positive impact."

Resources: May be tangible (space, money); intangible (time, buy-in); or human capital (trainers, staff)

Resource Needed	How Resource Can Be Obtained

Resource Available	Role or Benefit

Action Timeline:

Action	Time Frame	Puller Benefits/Risks
The specific activity you need to complete to move toward your solution. Consider listing activities in chronological order, from getting approval through carrying out the plan.	When will you work on or complete the action?	As the puller, you are fully involved in each action. What must you keep in mind?

act and consider the most effective means to structure your work. Let's take a moment to review the planner, and then we'll explore how to use it.

The Pull Planner is designed to give you an opportunity to think deeply about the outcomes you have for the situation you're trying to move forward. It also asks you to take stock. What resources are available that can help you with this work? What resources do you need? Finally, the planner has you consider the actions that need to be taken; the time in which they will occur; and then, most important, the benefits and risks for those involved. This last part is key with this force. Because everyone plays an active role, we need to continually focus on how everyone involved is doing. Unlike some of the other forces, this one needs to be completed from start to finish with no person left behind. We've also provided you with an example of a completed Pull Planner (Figure 4.3). Although our individual situations always differ, we can learn much from visualizing how others succeed and fail in their work. The example supplied may help you structure your own design.

Just as the Forces of Influence Leadership Matrix can help us determine where we tend to most readily live in our spectrum of forces, we can also see its value as a tool to help us differentiate our use of the forces. Following are some sentence starters that can lead into using a given force. As you'll see, pulls actively use elements of "we" as lead-ins for work, whereas the "we" is missing entirely from the realm of the shove. Also note the inquiry stance that a nudge takes on.

Figure 4.3 **Completed Pull Planner**

Challenge: The problem or challenge you want to solve	

Challenge: The problem or challenge you want to solve

Teachers are nervous about the 1:1 rollout but for different reasons. Some people need training on technical basics, some need strategies to use, some need apps, etc. The current professional development structure is one size fits all.

Desired Change: The resolution you desire

To provide short trainings on different topics instead of blanket mandatory PD. People should be able to choose the trainings they want to attend.

Impact (if/then): Your change written as an if/then statement. For example, "*If* we do XYZ, *then* ___ will be the positive impact."

If PD is personalized, then teachers will get the training they need without being bored or overwhelmed. If PD meets teachers' needs, then they will more likely accept and use 1:1 devices.

Resources: May be tangible (space, money); intangible (time, buy-in); or human capital (trainers, staff)

Resource Needed	How Resource Can Be Obtained
Trainers	Staff with experience, district trainers, state trainers (using local staff and district personnel will be cheaper/free and more feasible)
Teacher Needs	Send a short survey to teachers to see what topics they're most interested in
Time	When will trainings happen, and will teachers be paid per diem for participating?
Funding	Will trainers be paid? Will funding come from PD funds or PTA funds? Utilize existing faculty meeting or PD time, with different rooms for different topics.

Resource Available	Role or Benefit
Trained Staff	Three teachers are already using 1:1 effectively, and others are trained in apps. The media specialist can handle most technical stuff.
Space	Training with portions of the staff can happen in classrooms (because there are fewer people). The media center and computer labs are also open.
Credit	Setting up trainings through the district PD scheduler will give professional learning unit (PLU) credit to attendees and trainers.

(continued)

Figure 4.3 *continued*

Action Timeline:

Action	Time Frame	Puller Benefits/Risks
The specific activity you need to complete to move toward your solution. Consider listing activities in chronological order, from getting approval through carrying out the plan.	When will you work on or complete the action?	As the puller, you are fully involved in each action. What must you keep in mind?
1. Talk to teachers and other potential trainers and ask them to participate. Find out what presentations or trainings they feel comfortable leading and make a menu of options. Create a calendar of their availability.	April	Must be willing to help format and schedule presentations.
2. Find interested teachers. Get them to put forward suggestions about training to administration.	May	Must be willing to help teachers figure out when and how to approach administration.
3. Get administrative buy-in as well as leadership team and principal support.	Before PD planning for next year (June 1)	Must be willing to help the planning team and potentially work over the summer to get fall PD prepared.

- **Pull**
    - Let's try _____.
    - I think we should _____.
    - We're going to _____.
- **Push**
    - It would be great if you would _____.
    - I'd like to see you _____.
    - It's important for you to _____, and I'll be here to assist you if needed.
- **Shove**
    - You need to _____.
    - It's required that you _____.
    - _____ is expected of you.

- **Nudge**
  - I wonder _____.
  - Have you read _____?
  - Did you see _____?

Start Pulling

One big obstacle in the case of a pull is that those being pulled may not believe they can do the work themselves (and sometimes they may be right). So it's important that you use this force in a supportive manner. When engaging in the work with your pullees, emphasize your level of support throughout, how important this work is to you, and how you're going to engage in it together, from start to finish. It's also important to let others know that everyone has a say in how the work continues (so long as it continues moving forward). You should share the timeline you've drafted, understanding that with this force you must be open to the fact that others may help you shape that timeline further. Remember, in a pull, it's not acceptable to have loss of participation. This strategy is only truly successful if those who begin are also those who end. Here are some tips for making sure the pulling process begins productively:

- **Take the "reverse March" approach.** You know how the month of March comes in like a lion and goes out like a lamb? Take the opposite approach as you start your pulling work. Be soft in the way you start, be open to others' concerns and ideas, and don't initially pull too hard until everyone has a good grip. Then ratchet up the work until others feel they've hit their max. Just like a match of tug-of-war, the best pulls ebb and flow over the course of the initiative.

Meghan spent time working with a group of teachers to increase student talk in the classroom. She used her coaching position to introduce sentence stems and videos modeling the practice. Over the course of the year, Meghan worked with teachers in their professional learning communities to plan for student talk. She reviewed lesson plans with teachers and helped identify structures and questions that could prompt student talk. She provided teacher prompts and stems through printed reference pages and handy bookmarks to refer to during instruction. In one class, Meghan supported the implementation of student-led number talks, meeting with the teacher and students daily for a few weeks and brainstorming pacing that allowed time for student talk. Late in the year, teachers were asked to create videos of student talk in their classroom, and Meghan facilitated vertical team sharing and reflection. The practice moved from Meghan providing a lot of the background and information, to side-by-side work, to intense video reflection efforts.

- **Anticipate needs.** The best way to complete a pull is to make everyone happy. And the best way to make everyone happy is to give them what they need. A pull is first and foremost a happy force. Although all participants might not be happy throughout, the general idea is that everyone is pleased during the experience. (How else can we keep everyone actively involved?) And you, as the leader of the pull, have to be the happiest and most supportive of all!

A large part of Fred's role involves helping educators design professional learning opportunities for colleagues. One of the important steps Fred makes sure to include in his planning work is to ask lots of questions to understand where facilitators are coming from, what strengths they bring, and where they'll need the most support during the pull process. In this way, Fred can most effectively exert energy when needed, all the while relying on those he's partnered with to supply the energy when it makes the most sense.

Don't Let Up

The biggest challenge we've faced with pulls is that when you're pulling, you can never let up. Although we can rest from time to time by reducing the intensity, the process never stops until we're done. A refrain you've heard throughout this chapter is that the pull is the most intense force for everyone involved. Although it may not be the most intense for any given person, the sharing of that intensity does make it challenging for the integrity of the group. To pull for longer periods of time, here are three tips to keep in mind:

- **Celebrate.** Meeting benchmarks when pulling is a cause for celebration. Because you're all in the work together, taking time to celebrate even really small goals enables everyone to tighten their grip and pull harder.

A practice that Meghan's director of mathematics implements is a simple table share about what has gone well since the last coaches' meeting. Celebrations have included everything from increased test scores to improved relationships with teachers. Because all coaches feel a responsibility to elevate teaching and learning throughout the district, and all experience the day-to-day stress that comes with improving practices, these moments to celebrate provide simple joy and encourage pullers and pullees to keep going.

- **Know your limits.** This might seem to contradict the idea of not letting up. However, self-care for pullers is incredibly important. Because the work relies on the person maintaining that anchoring pull, the puller's health and well-being are intricately tied to the success of the work. When you're in this role, although it might feel uncomfortable to see your colleagues struggling throughout, remember that everyone involved has a monkey on their back; the person anchoring the work shouldn't bear more than his or her share. If the puller feels that all aren't involved, it makes sense to slow down; work with those who are struggling (moving back to anticipating needs, as necessary); and then pick back up when everyone is ready.

Sometimes it can feel as though we're attempting to force a boulder up a hill, all on our own. Several years ago, Fred was working with educators from across the state to put together a statewide blended learning initiative. Although the work was great, after a while, Fred found that he was working too hard for too many people. He realized that he needed to more explicitly share the thinking around the work that had to be done and hear how team members interpreted the work from their end. He decided to take a step back and let the pull unfold with a bit less guidance—in effect, letting others take on more responsibility. Because everyone was committed to the work, this "rebalancing" prompted other members of the team to lead tasks that they still had the energy for. Through the rest of this process, Fred was able to pull more effectively because responsibility was now more equally shared.

- **Take your time.** As you can no doubt see, a pull is rarely a fast force. The best pulls are relegated to work that can take a long time. Although this type of influence can often have long turnaround times, it can also lead to the greatest change. Because pulls can work with multiple people involved, the greatest impact can come from them. Don't rush it!

In putting together a complex learning institute, Fred had to spend a significant amount of time making sure that everyone was on the same page and was able to complete the tasks that were most aligned to their skill sets. Things were simply taking more time than expected. This meant that the institute had to be pushed back to a later date. Although it was difficult to admit that the work wasn't progressing as fast as they'd hoped, the ultimate goal was, in fact, a well-designed learning opportunity, and people just needed more time to accomplish this. When the institute did take place, a strong new partnership had been built and the facilitation was top-notch. This is a clear example of a well-executed pull that benefited by slowing down.

A key takeaway from this chapter? A pull is only as good as all those involved. Think carefully about the pulls you initiate, give them time to mature, and let them run their course. You'll know that the influencing is over when either everyone involved meets the goals originally set or you lose someone (or a bunch of someones) along the way. There's nothing wrong with stopping and either starting over again or investigating the use of another force. Remember that it's better to stop a misplaced force and go back to the start than it is to force a force that doesn't fit.

Roles and Relationships Check-In

Refer back to the Roles and Relationships Self-Assessment, Part I of which you filled out in Chapter 3 (see Figure 3.2, p. 52). Now that you have experience with pulls, which of the actions you've taken recently most align with a pull? If your actions don't align, consider whether a pull could have been effective. What small changes would have been necessary to shift your actions to this method of influence? Have you implemented pulls that weren't effective? If so, consider how you might revise your actions going forward to be more effective with a pull.

Let's now turn our attention in the chapter that follows to the next Force of Influence—the push.

Questions for Self-Reflection

- In your work, what types of scenarios seem the best fit for a pull?
- How does your planning fit in with your process for engaging in work and working with others?
- When considering the people with whom you work, what elements of the Pull Potential tool will enable you to identify good candidates for pulls? What elements will complicate things?
- Return to Part I of the Roles and Relationships Self-Assessment. What actions appear to be pulls? Note these and reflect on how your pull influenced the relationship.

Questions for Group Discussion

- What elements of effective collaboration would allow us to succeed in a pull? What are our pain points in this area?
- When it comes to initiating and sustaining pulls, what do we wonder about in terms of using this force in our organization?
- How can using a pull potentially benefit or damage a relationship? What planning can mitigate (we love this word!) any potential negative consequences?

5

The Push

There are times when we recognize that a colleague's potential for growth may one day outshine our own. And in those instances, it's up to us to help our colleagues realize their full potential and truly understand what they're capable of. These situations often require us to push people to their limits and help them overcome the obstacles that are currently in their way. Although it isn't always easy to put others into that position, it is easy to understand why it's so important. After all, if we believe in continuous improvement, then we have to prove to ourselves that we're capable of improving.

When Fred was serving as a science coordinator for his region, he spent time at state and national conferences. Having just started to find his way around Twitter, he was slowly building an understanding of the wider world of education and was beginning to make important connections with other science educators across the United States. At one conference, he met an extraordinarily capable science educator who was in the early stages of building an online presence. In the course of their discussions, she mentioned that she struggled with the fear of putting herself out there and sharing her ideas; she felt more comfortable sitting back and listening. Fred was likely one of a number of people who pushed her to become more at ease with serving as the leader it was clear she was. He encouraged her to share more ideas and questions online, and he offered his support as she became more comfortable. They partnered on a number of opportunities related to science, and, as Fred's role shifted, she continued to build her expertise and evolve her identity.

Today she's a sought-after science leader who works with one of the most highly regarded science education organizations in the United States. She and Fred no longer work together as closely because their roles have changed, yet he is thankful for all she has taught him. One often ignored element of a push is that the pushee may well grow beyond our ability to help further. Fred has enjoyed watching this science leader grow, and he is pleased at the idea that he was able to provide a bit of a push to help her get there.

The What

So now let's look at this force we call the push. We've all been pushed before, likely in a number of ways. These influence moves are truly active forces. We can see and feel them happening, and in the moment, they don't always feel so good (for either the pusher or the pushee). The best part about this move, though, is that it's done without intent to harm and with the promise of assistance through-out. There's a level of support that makes itself clear as the push unfolds. Let's look at how the people involved in a push influence the design of that force.

- **The pusher:** In a push, the person applying the force intends for the person on the receiving end to be out there on his or her own. What separates this force from its less welcoming sibling, the shove, is that in a push, the person applying the push will stay involved in a supporting manner. Think of it as the net below the tightrope. The tool is a passive support; the net is there *if* the acrobat needs it.

   In a push, the person pushing sets the receiver free with the understanding, either explicit or implicit, that the pusher is still there, ready to step in. The person pushing can't push well if he or she doesn't have some degree of expertise in the area the work is focused on. If the pusher can't supply the needed support, the influence move is doomed to fail. The pusher must have not only the background, but also the time to provide support for as long as it's needed. Lest the term *push* conjure up a quick motion force, consider it rather as something that can be slow and long term. Each pusher and pushee interaction looks different.

- **The pushee:** Being pushed by anyone—whether it's a friend, family member, or colleague—can be painful. It hurts to be pushed. It forces the pushee into a space he or she doesn't want to go; it's like being thrown into the spotlight before we've learned our lines. The push stresses relationships, because the person being pushed may initially feel abandoned. This can make it difficult for the person initiating the push, who actually does have the pushee's best interests in mind. Pushes only work if the pushee is ready for the change and is capable of taking the necessary steps.

During a hiring phase a number of years ago, Fred's supervisor wanted him to have experience closing out interview sessions with candidates they had not chosen to hire. The supervisor felt it was important for Fred to reach out to those interviewees who wouldn't be moving on and engage in the challenging conversations that often occur in these situations. While Fred recognized the importance of making these calls, he knew that they wouldn't be particularly enjoyable; no one ever wants to receive *or* deliver bad news. Although it was now Fred's responsibility to do this work, his supervisor let him know that if he got stuck or wanted to prepare elements of these phone calls in advance, she would be happy to provide support. Fred had just experienced being on the receiving end of a push, but he was confident to do this work on his own because he felt supported and invested in the process.

When we look back at our Forces of Influence Leadership Matrix (p. 45), we see what sets the push apart. Little preparation and direct effort are required on the front end of a push. Pushers use their knowledge of the pushee and of the person's past work and experiences as a guide to determine when to apply the strategy. However, this influence move does require significant support throughout. One can't simply rub one's hands together and walk away. Although it's easy to get started, a push is not necessarily as easy to complete.

The leadership matrix can also highlight some interesting aspects of force relatives. By "relatives," we mean that forces parallel to each other on a given axis have some key components in common. In the case of a push, the heavy involvement of the person applying this influence throughout the process resembles that of a pull. In both cases, the person initiating the force needs to have the time, energy, and experience to follow the work through to the end. Likewise, we can identify similarities between the shove and the push. In both of these cases, the forces require less work on the front end to initiate. And, in both cases, that lack of initial work potentially leaves those on the receiving end feeling scared, anxious, or angry at the outset.

Generally speaking, pushes are best employed when there's mutual respect between the person initiating and the one receiving. Jennifer Gonzalez (2016), author and editor of the "Cult of Pedagogy" blog, writes that we need to find the marigolds in our work. Marigolds are the people who embody all we want to become and all we envision in ourselves. In a push, this can work both ways. The person being pushed may recognize the tremendous expertise that a pusher can provide and may actively choose to be influenced by this person. On the flip side, the person applying the force may see something in the pushee that can help the organization or community and that might propel the person to great heights. This idea of "pushing for the marigolds" is important; because pushes require an investment to be successful, both the pushee and the pusher should value the relationship that exists between them.

A push is meant to bring out the best in others. A pull does this too, but it also brings out the best in oneself. There are times, however, when self-recognition is not the goal. For instance, a study by management consulting firm DDI (Weaver & Mitchell, 2012) showed that organizations that have effective leaders—those who know how to involve and support employees, provide sufficient feedback, and maximize efficiency, all while exhibiting respect, honesty, and empathy—are able to motivate close to 100 percent of their employees to do their best work. With ineffective leaders, that number hovers around 10 percent. And this brings us back to the push. When we recognize potential in others and provide them with the support they need to succeed in ways they thought impossible, we sow the seeds for long-term motivation.

The When

Pushes make the most sense when growth is required and the person on the receiving end merits the investment. Pushes are "in it for the long haul" forces. They showcase the belief that one person has in another through the support structure that the pusher puts into place. To that end, they require the initiator to have the time to push effectively.

In the grand scheme of a school calendar, for instance, pushes need to be instituted during periods in which the initiator can stay very much in tune with the receiver. A push started in May might not be effective if the pusher and pushee will be out of contact for the summer months. Likewise, a push by a mentor teacher may be ineffective for a mentee if that mentor must spend most of the time during a certain period working in a separate building.

In many cases, mentor programs and coaching structures follow a pusher/pushee design. The mentor or coach assesses the needs and wants of the pushee or mentee and develops a process to provide pushes throughout the partnership. During various activities, the mentor may assist with facilitation, but as the mentee's strengths grow, the mentor or pusher may simply serve as an observer. Although the responsibility of the change remains with the pushee, the responsibility of support remains with the pusher.

As we noted, pushes can only succeed when the person on the receiving end has a baseline of knowledge and skills. Here are some questions that the person applying the push can ask to quickly determine whether it's time for a push or whether a push is premature:

- **Is the potential pushee acclimated to the organization and ready to make a change?** If the pushee has yet to learn the nuances of a given organization and is at a heightened level of anxiety already, then a push may not be prudent. For the pushee to envision success, there has to be enough gas in the tank. When Meghan's district adopted a new mathematics program, teachers were stressed about pacing, new models, and addressing student needs. If Meghan had jumped in and tried to push for instructional changes as the teachers were struggling to learn the new program, they most likely would have resented her as a coach, displayed even less enthusiasm for the new curriculum, and seen Meghan as being out of touch with their needs.

- **Do I have the time (and energy) to devote to the push and pushee?** Because the initiation of the push is easy enough, it can seem like the entire process may be smooth sailing. Pushers need to keep in mind that once a push is initiated, it may require a sustained level of ongoing support.

- **Am I the right person to provide the push?** A push requires mutual respect and a willingness to put the relationship between the pusher and the pushee in an uncomfortable space initially. As with some of the other forces, if the wrong people are matched up, the force may be doomed from the start. How can you determine if you're a good match for a potential pushee? Consider the strength of your relationship and how well you know each other and for how long. Ask yourself whether you have significant expertise in the area in which the person needs to be pushed and whether you can handle conflict and still remain supportive. If you have a strong relationship with someone, significant expertise in the area of focus, and developed skills in being both supportive and critical, then a push is likely a good choice.

It's important to be open, however, to reevaluating one's position as a pusher. When providing support to one of his colleagues, Fred realized that although they had a positive relationship, a different staff member would be a better fit. Along with his supervisor, Fred met with this other person to set up the push that would go into effect.

Let's take a moment to explore the positives and negatives of this approach.

- **The positives:**
  - Pushes, by their nature, tend to be a light touch. It doesn't take much energy for the pushee to realize that the force was implemented for good reasons.
  - One of the biggest obstacles to change is inertia. We often need a push to get things moving (or to get things to stop). Because we're often blind to our own inertia, receiving a push from others can help us overcome obstacles we didn't recognize initially.

- – Success always feels better when we know we've achieved it as a result of our hard work. Although support is only a request away in a push, the fact that we're on our own can motivate us to see things through.
- • **The negatives:**
  - – Even the best relationships break under certain strain. A push is impossible to carry out unless you're willing to test the strength of a relationship.
  - – Pushes don't have a timeline. Like with a pull, the one initiating the force commits to providing support through to the end. Sometimes this is a long, long time.
  - – A push is transparent. Everyone can recognize what's going on, and no one will miss the fact that the pusher did, in fact, push the pushee.

So think of the push as one of our favorite ice cream flavors, rocky road. It's definitely rough and choppy to start, as the initiator and the receiver navigate the force, but once everything settles down, smooths out, and the pushee grows, it becomes clear how great the combination can be.

The Why

Exploring the "why" of a push is important for understanding whether the time is right to push or whether it's time to investigate other choices. Let's say we want to get teachers to use exit ticket data in mathematics to inform instruction and that we're going to use a push to help make that happen. Let's consider that push from a variety of perspectives to investigate why these moves are used and how ongoing support can vary.

I'm an Administrator

The why: An administrator might want to push teachers to use a certain practice, and a strong administrator is part of the learning process. A willingness on the part of the administrator to stay involved will go a long way toward ensuring lasting implementation and, therefore, lasting impact. In addition, teachers don't want mandates thrown at them without support in time, funding, or application. Administrators can provide that support through a push.

The support: An administrator who wants to push for teachers to use exit ticket data might present the idea in a professional learning community (PLC). Although the administrator would tell teachers what they need to implement, he or she wouldn't come prepared with exit tickets or data recording pages, or even share the initial thinking about how to proceed. Ongoing support from the administrator might include setting aside time to review data, joining the PLCs as they meet, or even sending teachers to professional learning opportunities so they can learn more about how to implement the change.

I'm a Coach

The why: A coach wants to engage with teachers in using exit tickets to make sure they're implementing the practice correctly. Because coaches are often the middle person between a district or administrative shove and actual teacher implementation, they're in a perfect position to push instructional practice.

The support: In the push to use exit tickets to inform instruction, a coach could share documents to support teachers in collecting data, but the coach wouldn't initially create any new products for the teachers. Once teachers have committed to the idea, the coach might provide ongoing feedback and help teachers select the exit tickets to use. The coach might also provide guidance to teachers when looking at student work, help collect and record information, and help determine the most effective instruction. Some coaches, if requested, may even help teach the intervention if it's clear the teacher needs support in this area. If, on the contrary, a coach attends trainings, develops resources, or provides professional development *before* teachers have committed to working with exit ticket data, he or she has crossed over into the pull quadrant; at that point, the coach would either have to reevaluate his or her use of influence or change the desired outcomes.

I'm a Teacher

The why: Teachers might recognize the need for implementing a specific practice or have experience with a successful strategy that they want to share with their grade level. They might also hope to influence an administrator in allowing a new practice to be used throughout the school. Teachers offering solutions are a welcome commodity, but they usually have to walk the walk if they hope to talk the talk (and gain support and respect). A push is a great tool for teachers because they can bring ideas to the table without having to invest a lot of time and effort on the front end, and then they're in a perfect position to work with the project as support is needed.

The support: Let's say a teacher suggests to an administrator that using exit ticket data to drive instruction has been a successful practice in his classroom. He offers to work with his grade-level team to select common student work samples and create recording forms. Teachers bring in outside resources and attend trainings to help support the effort. They coordinate work with a coach and share experiences with other teachers to help grow the practice. The teacher who has had success with this practice shares success stories and challenges and is available to the rest of the team for support and to answer any questions. Unlike in a pull, the teacher would only get involved if the rest of the team needed assistance.

How can you determine if a push is needed? If you find you have to frontload the work before diving in, you're likely looking at a pull. If you're able to get buy-in for the idea before attacking any of the work, or if the people you're working with are prepared to lead the work on their own, you're more likely looking at a push. If you find yourself in the position of telling someone else what to do and then handing off all the work, then you might not be using either a push or a pull. Remember, a key component of both push and pull is participating in ongoing support to bring the change to completion.

How can we take stock of the type of force needed in a given situation? Look at the Force Factor Worksheet shown in Figure 5.1. To use it, simply describe the action or change you hope to accomplish and then list the activities that will need to happen both before you apply the force and during the process that ensues. Finally, circle those activities that you're willing to be the lead on. Use the Force Factor table at the bottom of the worksheet to compare how your circled actions relate to the choice of a force.

Figure 5.1 **Force Factor Worksheet**

To take stock of the type of force needed, describe the action or change you hope to accomplish, then list the activities needed for that action or change to take place. Circle the activities that you are willing to be the lead on. Then compare those circled actions with the Force Factor Table at the bottom of the worksheet.

Action or Change Desired:	
Needed Prior to Implementation	**Needed During and Throughout Implementation**

Force Factor Table

Push	Pull
I don't want to put in much effort before we agree to the action, but I'm committed to seeing the action through and doing the work after we agree to take it on.	I need to put in work on the front end, and I'm committed to seeing the action through and doing the work after we agree to take it on.
Shove	**Nudge**
I don't want to put in much effort before we agree to the action, and I need someone else to complete the work. I might oversee the work from a detached vantage point.	I'm willing to put in work on the front end, but I won't complete the work once things get going. I want to work behind the scenes to effect change.

The How

One advantage of a push is that it doesn't need a lot of preparation. And clearly, to get more buy-in, it's important to have some authority or expertise in the focus area. Although a push may feel authoritative at first, the expertise or respected experience of a colleague often makes the difference between a successful push and one that isn't appreciated.

You don't need to spend a ton of time and effort researching or building materials for your push, but it does make great sense to "think forward" and consider its impact. We can do that through using a SWOT analysis, a quick tool often used in business to assess *strengths*, *weaknesses*, *opportunities*, and *threats* for a given action, change, or goal. By taking a few minutes to write down what you hope to gain from your push and what might stand in your way, you'll be better prepared to use a push—or to walk away from one force in favor of another. Considering the possible pushback goes a long way to solidifying (or abandoning) your push and clarifying your goals.

I Didn't Sign Up for This

There may come a time when you find yourself in a push you didn't plan for. You might have tossed out an errant idea or mentioned something you'd seen or heard, and all of a sudden you're the champion for whatever is out on the table. We're often so invested in our work and in the good of an organization that we say "sure!" when asked to take on a task, without taking the time to consider all the implications.

No matter how you got there, you proposed something that you're now committed to seeing through, so look for the silver lining. Your unintentional push has the potential to become an unintentional success. It doesn't really matter how you got yourself involved in this influence move; the key is to carry it through to completion.

When a teacher in Meghan's school was asked to join a leadership team training about metacognition, her reaction was "Why not?" When she got to the training, she realized not only that this would be new learning for her, but also that she was expected to go back to the school and help implement the approach with others—all because she said OK, never realizing what it would entail. The teacher suddenly acquired the opportunity to become a schoolwide leader, along with the responsibility of influencing others.

A Voice from the Field

One of the most rewarding aspects of my career as the director of curriculum and instruction in a regional agency has been to create and sustain the Curriculum Council, a professional learning community (PLC) for curriculum and instruction leaders in the region. The PLC has continued to thrive since it began more than 25 years ago. One of the secrets to its success is that members are responsible for facilitating monthly learning sessions.

At the end of each school year, Council members reflect on what they learned and identify the focus of the learning for the next school year. With a little encouragement from me, members volunteer to cofacilitate one of the sessions. (Encouragement consists of requesting them to do this, expressing my sincere belief that they will do a great job, and offering support.) This is a high-stakes activity because the Council has a strong reputation for being a vibrant learning community; members don't want to disappoint other members when it's their turn to lead a session.

A "push" is a nice way to describe the support I provide. When it's a member's turn to lead, I send them a friendly reminder that their session will be coming up in the next few weeks. I request a brief description of their plans to include on the Curriculum Council agenda and in the e-mail I send to Council members a week before the meeting. I let them know that they can call me to discuss their ideas for leading the session and that I would be happy to give them feedback. Some members feel comfortable designing the session on their own and just let me know what they plan to do. Others seek my support in designing the session, and these calls often involve me asking questions to support members as they hash out their plans. In the end, Council members lead the session, and by doing so, they strengthen the PLC through collective ownership and leadership.

—**Marla Gardner**
Former Director of Curriculum and Instructional Services, Putnam/Northern Westchester Board of Cooperative Educational Services (BOCES) Yorktown Heights, NY

Take a few moments to consider Gardner's use of the push in the Curriculum Council. How did she use it? Would you have pushed in the same way? Would a pull work in this type of situation? Why or why not?

Roles and Relationships Check-In

Once again, refer back to the Roles and Relationships Self-Assessment (see Figure 3.2, p. 52). Now that you're more familiar with pushes, which of your activities align with that approach? If you find your actions don't align with a push, consider when a push might have been effective. What small changes would have been required to create a push? Have you implemented pushes that weren't effective? Consider how you might revise your actions going forward to make such a push more effective.

A push, then, enables people to take the lead in their own growth, knowing that support is available should it be needed. In our next chapter, we'll shift to a force that contains some similarities to a push, but key differences make it necessary in its own right.

Questions for Self-Reflection

- What aspects of a push are most relevant to your current role?
- How might you initiate a push to up the chances of success?
- How would you use a push with those you work closely with? What aspects of those relationships would you need to consider?
- What areas of expertise do you have that might position you as a pusher?
- Are there cases where you might be able to push but wouldn't choose to do so?

Questions for Group Discussion

- In what ways are initiating pushes and pulls similar? In what ways are they different?
- Can pushes be used effectively in groups larger than pairs? Why or why not?
- What are the advantages and disadvantages of the different roles involved in implementing a push?
- How might pushes be better received from a peer than from someone in an authoritative stance?

6

The Shove

Mentoring new teachers is often akin to coaching; you help hone their skills through guided practice and modeling. But there comes a day when new teachers have to be on their own. . . .

Meghan had a student teacher who was happy to do the ancillary teaching tasks—like cutting out laminations, checking homework folders, and running copies—but when it came to standing in front of the class, she used every avoidance strategy in the book. She "forgot" her lesson plan, didn't want to "mess up" the math, or showered Meghan with praise in an attempt to not teach. Eventually, Meghan had to tell her what she would be teaching on Tuesday and let her go it alone. Meghan wasn't going to plan for her, coteach, or jump in and save her. It was time for the student teacher to teach, to either sink or swim.

The lesson started out rocky. The pacing was slow, and students were becoming increasingly disengaged. They were having a hard time visualizing this tough fractions concept. When the student teacher pulled out colored candy pieces and distributed them, Meghan nearly balked, thinking the class was going to go from sleepy to a sugar-infused high in no time. But to her surprise, the student teacher recovered and made the lesson hands-on in a way that Meghan had never considered. When all was said and done, the student teacher was able to complete a quality lesson. Certainly, the student teacher had much to work on, but she needed the initial shove to get started—and she needed Meghan to be hands-off. Shoving her into teaching too early would have overwhelmed her and resulted in failure, but waiting too long would have robbed her of the experience she needed to build on. A well-placed directive got her started on the way to a solid first year of teaching.

The What

Let's take a quick trip back to physics class. Sir Isaac Newton instructed us in some very important laws of motion, the first one being this: an object at rest will stay at rest unless acted on by an outside force. As we've noted in previous chapters, there's a certain level of initial involvement and ongoing support inherent in all forces. When you push a snow shovel along a snowy walkway, the shovel doesn't remain in motion by itself. You have to accompany the shovel and then dump out the snow.

Such is the way with pushes; there's a level of ongoing involvement inherent in the force. The same is true for a pull; you can pull your friend to the dance floor, and, by so doing, you're kind of committed to dance along with him or her. A shove, by contrast, capitalizes on the fact that sometimes we need others to do all the work; we don't want to get the work started or see it through to completion. Consider a sled. With little preparation or forethought, you can shove the sled down the hill, and then it continues without you. This is how shoves work in a professional context as well. You can direct the action with little work on your part, either before or after the process takes off.

The shove operates in a quadrant where low initial involvement and low ongoing support coincide. And although this approach to getting things done can feel task-oriented at times, research about transformative leadership notes that directive leadership can actually be desirable. Directive leaders are adept at moving followers out of crisis, giving instructions and setting expectations, establishing timelines and performance standards, and offering radical solutions (Bass & Riggio, 2006).

The When

If you want to go sledding, you need a robust and forceful action to get started. A less powerful act than a shove just wouldn't have the same effect. Shoves are also time based. If an action is needed quickly, then acting with a decisive move makes sense. The directive to turn in your lunch selection before 11:00 a.m. ensures that what you want to eat will be available to you later on in the day. No one is going to guide you in this decision, and if you can't do what's required (turn in your lunch order), then you have to deal with the consequences (insert "least favorite lunch food item" here). When deadlines are at stake, we tend to operate in the shove quadrant.

We can't operate in any one quadrant at all times. Nor can we have a building full of one type of operator. A person who always acts in the pull quadrant is likely to burn out from being involved in everything at every level. An abundance of pulls may feel like change is slow and draining. Meanwhile, an abundance of shoves is likely to lead to clear direction without true investment, as well as feelings of resentment from those on the receiving end. Change might feel fast, but sustainability may suffer.

To better set the context for a shove, let's look at some of the characteristics and consequences of each of the forces:

- **Pull**
  - The person being pulled may sense the need for change, but he or she doesn't feel a need to rush or for immediate action.
  - A pull works best when the person pulling can put in a lot of time developing the pull and participating in follow-up.
  - People who pull are likely to be coworkers or friends who are highly invested in the person they wish to influence.
- **Push**
  - There's a sense of urgency for the person being pushed to begin action, but results may take a while to develop.
  - A push works best when the action can develop over time.
  - People who push are likely to be coaches, who follow up with support over time.
- **Shove**
  - There's a sense of urgency for both the person shoving and the person being shoved.
  - A shove works best when action is immediately necessary.
  - Shoves are likely to come from a position of authority, and they have drastic relationship implications.

- **Nudge**
  - The person being nudged may feel pressure or the need for change, but action can take time to develop.
  - A nudge works best when influence can be subtly applied or action is not required immediately.
  - Nudges can be employed by a person in any position, but on the receiving end, they feel particularly friendly to those without titles or authoritative positions.

Thomas Guskey's (2002) theory of change posits that getting a successful outcome from actions, which may or may not have been mandated, will result in a shift in beliefs and attitudes. Once attitudes and beliefs change, it's more likely that the action that spurred the change will be repeated. A shove aligns well with Guskey's theory of change in that the action itself can be mandated. Consider the adoption of a new math curriculum. The district decides on a curriculum to implement, and then teachers are told to adhere to it. The program results in positives: supportive materials for teachers, less piecing together of supplemental resources, and improved student achievement. Teacher beliefs and attitudes about adopting the new curriculum begin to shift, and they're more likely to continue implementation.

By contrast, Desimone (2009) presents a different picture. According to his view of change, if we plan to take action, attitudes and beliefs have to change *first*. If that's the case, then no amount of shoving will build buy-in; only compliance will come from shoving alone. If those same teachers are directed to use that new math curriculum and they haven't developed any buy-in along the way, they're less likely to implement programs effectively. We can make sure that a book lands in someone's hands, but we may find it's more difficult to overcome displaced attitudes and beliefs, especially if results aren't immediately obvious.

Does that mean that using a shove is never appropriate? Not at all. Shoves will work best when direct action and timeliness are key. They're less likely to be successful if attitudes and beliefs are out of line with the desired action.

Thinking back to our physics example, Newton provided us with an insightful third law as well. It states that for every action, there is an equal and opposite reaction. If you shove a friend into a pool, there will be some kind of response. It may be the friend laughs it off and pulls you in—or you may have just lost a really good friend (well, maybe not *that* good of a friend, if all it took to destroy the friendship was a shove into a pool). So, knowing the potential for a shove to feel, well, shove-like, why is it sometimes the necessary and powerful force we need to employ?

The Why

We've all had the experience of working with others who need to be directed. Chances are, there have probably been times in our own lives where we needed a good shove as well. It isn't simply about getting work done. It's also about putting people in a position where they have to make a call. Can they accomplish the task in front of them or not? A shove is as much about helping others prove to themselves that they can be successful as it is about proving it to someone else. It's both the most forceful force and also potentially the most self-fulfilling.

Fred remembers being shoved quite a bit during his student teaching. At the time it felt bad, and Fred regularly left school wondering why his cooperating teacher was hanging him out to dry. But once he started teaching, he understood. If he hadn't had the opportunity to fly on his own, he wouldn't have been able to handle the challenges he faced as a classroom teacher. If we're able to do what we've been shoved to do, then we've truly done it—and on our own, as well.

Of course, not all instances end so happily. Meghan has worked with teachers who leave the school or profession altogether because they felt overly directed by administrators. Frustrated with a lack of change or feeling they need to be assertive, administrators may issue directives that teachers feel unable or unwilling to handle. There's a delicate balance between allowing autonomy and directing change, particularly when it comes to shoves. In instances like this, neither the school, administrator, nor teacher benefit. Besides being the most fulfilling of the forces, shoves can also be the most agonizing. When we fail during a shove, we fail hard. And we may never be able to recover.

So, knowing the high risk and high reward quotient of a shove, it's fair to ask, why bother? To understand that, we'll explore two different situations where a shove can be truly beneficial.

When People Won't Move

Relationships are hard. Any number of complications can make it difficult to work with others. At times, one of the members in a relationship may simply refuse to make the change that is necessary for his or her own betterment or for that of the people involved. Why would anyone refuse to make changes that will end up helping in the long run? Although sometimes these responses stem from the relationship itself (feeling like an unequal partner, not agreeing with the direction the relationship is taking, and so on), at other times action refusal is about something outside the relationship's control; the person simply may not be in the right place or space to make change.

Inaction may be OK in certain instances, but it's never OK when it leads to paralysis. One thing we know about learning is that it requires constant change. If we want the best for those we serve, then we have to be willing to work toward continuous improvement, and that means never stopping in our work. When paralysis does set in and a relationship or community may suffer as a result, a shove may be precisely what is needed to help move the work forward and make it clear that inaction can never be a state of being. Much like jumping into an unexpectedly cold pool can bring all our senses to the forefront, a directive can say, "I care so much about you that I need you to do this now, to move out of your comfort zone and grow."

When Stress Is Helpful

A shove also has the added benefit of using the power of positive stress to help others take action. A study conducted at the University of California, Berkeley (Kirby et al., 2013), found that an increased level of stress hormones in rats led to enhanced neural functioning and learning. Another study the same year (Crum, Salovey, & Achor, 2013) found that students who were naturally inclined to see stress as helpful had lower hormone changes when presented with a stressful situation than others who tended to see stress as, well, stressful, and they were more likely to seek feedback on their work.

As the research shows, in some cases, stress can actually empower us to take action and make change. Applying just the right amount of stress can show a person just what he or she is capable of. Of course, like many things, this approach only works in moderation. If we dial up the stress too quickly or make it too intense, we can cause people to shut down and make it seem as though we're out to get them or we lack caring and empathy.

So stress itself is neither good nor bad. Rather, it's the degree and intensity that determine whether it will bolster someone's abilities or stifle them. For example, let's say we're working with colleagues on incorporating a new technology tool into our practice. The tool is new; no one has much experience with it. The questions that colleagues are asking and their reluctance to use the tool show that their initial level of stress is high. So rather than continue to shove at that moment in time, it would be far more sensible to give everyone a few days to view the tutorials and watch the sample teaching demonstration. Then, at the next session, everyone would be far more comfortable with diving into tool usage. Notice that the directive is still there—our colleagues are still expected to use this technology tool—but now it feels more balanced. Everyone will still need to learn on their own and rise to the occasion, but not at the expense of having everyone throw up their hands and not even make an attempt. Not too hot, not too cold, just right.

So using a shove can be tricky. If you choose this strategy, you must be mindful of the stress it may induce. Let's see how Principal Johnson handled that.

A Voice from the Field

I've always wondered what school would be like if classes sparked student curiosity daily. I envisioned exciting students to the point where they would pester their parents to buy materials to beta-test an idea. I set out to create such an environment. Little did I know how challenging the journey would become.

To achieve my vision, teachers needed to move from a mindset of "I have to create my own curriculum" to "I *get* to create my own curriculum." Our staff had no problem buying in, but the actual instructional change was easier said than done. Teachers initially found inquiry-based teaching very stressful. As a result, they fell back into their comfort zone of a traditional lesson style.

I realized that adult behaviors were preventing successful implementation. Some teachers were fast adopters but faltered when facilitating inquiry for the first time. Others tried to wait it out as just another initiative. Surprisingly, some teachers were outright defiant about implementing the approach. I knew we had to make some sweeping and difficult adjustments. I assembled our campus teacher leaders and worked with them to chart our future course with inquiry-based learning. The collective resolution was stunning. We agreed to require teachers to teach using inquiry-based methods 75 percent of the time.

At the next staff meeting, I shared the collective mandate. You could have heard a pin drop. Some teachers were processing, and others were seething. Over the next six months, the key to our success hinged on our administrative staff taking a posture of "requiring." We had suggested, hinted, and pushed—and now we needed to shove our reluctant staff in the direction we needed them to go. Teachers were required to use common vocabulary, employ a common lesson structure, and implement formative assessments of student learning.

As an administrative team, we gained synergy and renewed focus because every time we entered a classroom we were looking for vocabulary, structure, and formative assessment. Reaching consensus with buy-in is often ideal, but when you're struggling to get movement in the direction that you need, *requiring* may be the best choice. Ultimately, we were able to prove that inquiry-based learning could spark curiosity within students and contribute to closing achievement gaps. Even with an implementation dip, we still outperformed the district in almost every category, and we went on to greater achievement from there.

—Brandon Johnson
Principal, Lake Ridge High School
Mansfield, TX

In Johnson's case, using a shove came as a result of other forces not working. The directive wasn't negative; the principal promoted best practices and helped to override fears and hesitations. He put in some work with his leadership team, impressing on them and, in turn, on his teachers the seriousness of the situation and forcing the timeline to move ahead. The result? Teachers now use inquiry-based practices, and the leadership team has a unified way to assess these practices.

To help determine whether the time is right to apply a shove and what the potential level of stress acceptance might be, we offer the Stress Test shown in Figure 6.1 as a guide.

We recognize the challenge of a shove. Although we always want those we serve to be empowered to make change, there are times when it's absolutely necessary to move a process forward. In these instances, using a shove becomes the best hope for a positive resolution and the only way to overcome inertia.

Figure 6.1 **Stress Test**

Put a check in either the Yes or the No box to indicate whether you agree or disagree with the statement. At the end, if you have more Yes boxes checked than No boxes, then a shove—and the stress it often leads to—may be appropriate to put into practice.

Description	Yes	No
The person you wish to influence has been plagued by inaction for a significant period of time.	✓	
The relationship with the person has suffered as a result of the person's inaction.	✓	
A change is imperative and needs to be made sooner rather than later.		✓
The person has a strong work ethic.		✓
The person often chooses to rise to the occasion rather than give up.		✓
The person has a strong self-concept and believes in his or her ability to do good work.	✓	
The person is logical and tends to be levelheaded in times of challenge.		✓
The person doesn't get discouraged when things don't go his or her way.		✓

A Voice from the Field

As assistant superintendent for curriculum, I've been reluctant to make excessive use of positional authority to initiate change or mobilize people to action. This stems from my belief that effective educators build organizational capacity through empowerment first. That said, it's also true that strategic leaders must recognize how to directly influence others to establish urgency for an initiative or orchestrate expertise and resources toward defined outcomes.

Our middle school has a reputation for being a safe, welcoming, and student-friendly learning environment. The school was largely distinguished by one program, an advanced mathematics curriculum that has raised achievement levels for all students over many years. Not surprisingly, the school reflects its veteran principal: it's purposefully structured to maximize efficiencies, and it's highly effective in delivering on established expectations.

This was a classic "good to great" challenge for the school and, in particular, for the principal, who had led the school for more than a decade. It was clear that the school culture had internalized a "good enough" mindset. After a series of ineffective nudges, I realized that both the school and the principal needed a shove.

Following the successful adoption of the International Baccalaureate (IB) Diploma Program at our high school, I determined that the best strategy for mobilizing the middle school would be to advance our application to the IB Middle Years Program. It offered a comprehensive and aspirational framework for improvement that was designed to be a coherent, vertically articulated, and performance-based instructional framework. It also presented a host of challenges: cost, extensive professional development, and holistic curriculum and assessment redesign, as well as significant structural changes.

My original intent was to establish the need for adoption of the program and guide the principal to this realization through a series of influence moves. I was met with passive resistance. I realized that the transformational shifts that I believed were necessary would require an intervention that was more forceful and direct, one that leveraged my positional authority as well as the trust and respect established during my long-standing relationship with the principal.

So I set the process in motion by initiating a formal self-study, advocating funds for professional development, meeting with faculty, and designing an action plan with a timeline. I offered the principal a choice. He could either adopt the IB Middle Years Program or propose an alternative instructional improvement vision for his school.

The school is now in its second year of implementation. The principal is highly engaged in leading the adoption of the program, the school is demonstrating energy and passion for the challenging work of redefining learning, and students and parents are showcasing a new level of pride in their school.

On reflection, my decision to shove the principal to action was born out of frustration, experience, and diagnosis. It was calculated and carefully researched. I considered the risks and assessed the readiness of the faculty, the

parents, and the students. I prepared district-level leaders
for the work and accounted for the disequilibrium that the
adoption would likely bring to bear on the school. And, no
less important, I put my trust and confidence in the leadership capacity of my colleague, the school principal, to step
up and into this transformational opportunity.

—Michael Greenfield
*Assistant Superintendent for Curriculum,
Harrison Central School District
Harrison, NY*

Greenfield made good use of the shove and got great results.
Let's now look at some strategies and processes that can ensure success when you use this approach.

The How

Shoving can sometimes be emotionally difficult. Recall that pushes
and pulls offer support over the long term; directives, however, rarely
have initial or ongoing support. As you can no doubt imagine, a
shove can be pretty easy logistically. It's dealing with the "how" of
moving forward from a shove that can be more difficult.

Shoving basically involves informing your resistant colleague
that a change must be made—and that it rests on him or her to
make that change. Because you are, in effect, at a point of no return,
it's unlikely to leave anyone feeling good. After all, the first move
will be a difficult conversation. With that in mind, here are some
strategies to help you use this pressure sensitively and fairly.

Engage in the Conversation on Their Turf

If you're the one applying the pressure, you may leave the inter-action with little more than a bruised ego. For the colleague being shoved, however, the aftermath will be worse. The least you can do is take the environmental stress out of the conversation by meeting in your colleague's classroom, office, or safe space. Any way to reduce his or her stress is worthy of consideration.

Use Active Listening Strategies

Those being shoved will likely be emotional from the outset. After all, they've just been dealt an ultimatum, and nobody likes those. Active listening strategies can help defuse anger and reduce tension. And although they can't take away the pain of a forceful directive, they can reduce the initial sting. Active listening strate-gies include turning to face the person you're speaking with; para-phrasing ("So what I hear you saying is . . ."); and asking clarifying questions ("Can you tell me more about why you feel this request is so troubling?"). These strategies help humanize discourse that is challenging. As Stone, Patton, and Heen write in their excel-lent book *Difficult Conversations* (1999), "Identity challenges can be earth-shattering, particularly when a conversation can cause you to relinquish a cherished aspect of how you see yourself" (pp. 113–114). Because shoves are always about moving people to see how they can improve, it's no wonder they often lead people to question their value and self-worth. By using active listening strategies, you can make it clear to your colleague that although they must take the way forward independently, you acknowledge and understand the situation.

Welcome Emotion

A shove brings up tremendous emotional baggage. Your colleague will probably react emotionally, with anger and frustration, and you'll probably experience strong emotions as you express your own understanding, concern, and empathy. And although you may also feel your own anger and frustration from putting this force in place, it's a bit like getting upset when you rub pollen all over yourself and become a target for bees. It's logical, but there's also a bit of "well, what did you expect"?

Once you've put the pressure on, there's little to do but wait and see what happens. This isn't exactly easy either, as our inclination as human beings is to help one another out. Of course, once you make the decision to shove, chances are, you're coming to the end of a struggle that has already gone on too long.

When a colleague makes a change based on this force, you (or whoever did the shoving) need to welcome the work. Remember Goldilocks and the "just right" principle? A shove followed too quickly by another shove can shift the "just right" balance in the relationship. If that happens, you'd need to use another force to shift the balance back. This pressure often strains relationships, so even if your colleague makes the change necessary, don't expect relationships to return to what they were. Although this can hurt, not acting can have worse results.

In Meghan's coaching role, she balances the forces and relies on strong relationship building to encourage teachers to use best practices. Occasionally, a shove damages relationships. In order to have a productive data review, Meghan told teachers that they would have to print and bring their own data ready to examine to each meeting—no ifs, ands, or buts. Not liking the direction they were given, the teachers decided to bow out of any more data meetings with Meghan. The coaching relationship suffered a considerable setback, and the failed interaction left neither Meghan nor the teachers in a better place to serve students.

Understand That Some May Be Unwilling to Comply

So what if your colleague can't meet the requirements? Then, in fairness, it's time to remove him or her from the situation that led to the shove in the first place. Once that happens, it's only normal to expect that the relationship will never be the same. Also, understand that although some colleagues put under this pressure won't agree with this change initially (and may never agree), it's likely that the shove proved why a change had to be made. Clearly, we want to retain teachers, yet there are instances where our requests are completely within reason and should be heeded. An administrator might require lesson plans, punctuality, or professional dress. If a teacher is unwilling to meet those expectations, maybe it's best for all involved that the teacher find a different environment more in sync with his or her needs. Yes, relationships may change and break, but likely for the benefit of everyone involved.

When the Tables Are Turned

What if *you* end up on the receiving end of a shove? How can you respond? Being directed is a part of our lives, and sometimes it's precisely what we need to improve. With that in mind, we would ask you to consider a few things as you navigate situations in which the more intense pressure is on you.

- **Understand the shove.** Shoves are rarely nefarious, and they often can be easily explained. Do your best to balance emotion with rationality, and ask questions that are more about discovery than about blame. If, of course, you *do* understand why the shove is occurring, own it. Questioning a change in practice that you know you should be making will only make the experience worse for everyone involved.
- **Make a decision.** Although being shoved might make you feel powerless, that's never the case. You always have a choice. You can work toward the change or work to avoid it. Usually, working toward the change is the better choice. That said, there are times when you know it won't solve the underlying problem. Either way, you have to make a decision whether to change or not. And that decision is in your lap.
- **Accept responsibility (and the consequences).** If you're getting shoved, then likely you've already been involved in a challenging situation. You have to now accept responsibility for what you've done before (and for what you'll do in response). This does two things: first, it enables the person giving direction to feel some relief; second, it proves that although you may have caused some friction, you're willing to reflect, improve, and make things right.

Roles and Relationships Check-In

In which of your relationships are you more likely to shove? When have you gotten shoved? Refer back to the Roles and Relationships Self-Assessment (see Figure 3.2, p. 52) and read through your roles and relationships to determine whether you've directed others with a shove. Keep in mind that directives are sometimes necessary, so don't worry if this seems to be your go-to force. If you find your actions don't align with a shove, consider when it could have been effective. Are certain roles more prone to initiating shoves than others? Why?

In this chapter, we considered the most forceful of forces. In the next, we'll look at a force that demands only the subtlest of touches—the nudge.

Questions for Self-Reflection

- What aspects of your current context lend themselves to shoves? Which ones don't? Why?
- Consider a time when you shoved and it backfired. Was there some way to still use a shove but change the outcome? What could you have done differently?
- How might you position a shove to maximize results without compromising relationships?
- Are there instances where you could have initiated a shove but you held off? Why?
- Consider a time when you received a shove that went well. How was the shove positioned so it resulted in a positive outcome?

Questions for Group Discussion

- What aspects of a shove are positive?
- What makes us more likely to accept a shove?
- How can we develop a culture in which an appropriate shove feels welcome?
- Are we more likely to accept a shove from certain individuals? What characteristics of that person make us more accepting and open to a shove?
- What are our hard stops? Where and when would we not accept a shove, and why?

7

The Nudge

We've all had the privilege of working for supervisors who don't match our ways of learning and leading. They give us an opportunity to grow, often much faster than we might have otherwise done, and they often build our capacity to use a subtle force—the nudge.

Back in the beginning of his career, Fred worked with a supervisor who believed that no one else was ever right, that it was his way or the highway. Fred slowly learned that he had to be more subtle in his work with this person and that the only way he could ever accomplish anything for his department was by using outside resources to sway the supervisor's opinion. There was no way this person would ever listen to Fred and Fred alone, regardless of how much expertise or experience he had.

In one situation that involved participating in a lesson study trial, Fred shared a number of resources from well-respected educational organizations with the supervisor to show how valuable this experience was and why it would benefit the department to give time to the teachers to engage in this work. Fred offered to discuss it with the supervisor, and although the supervisor wasn't one for talking education, he was willing to explore the resources shared and ultimately became convinced that it actually would be good for the department to engage in this practice.

And they did. And the learning they all took from it was well worth the effort that went into planning for the nudge.

The What

Remember when you changed course on a decision on the basis of an interaction with a peer? Sure, it's possible that the person gave you some great advice or told you the steps to take to help you shift your thinking. It's also possible you were nudged, without your knowing, into making a different decision.

What's the difference? Quite a bit, actually. Whereas advice is something that is explicitly given with the hope of influencing decision making, a nudge is more subtle, and sometimes even subliminal. A nudge often influences people's choices without their full awareness of that fact. This subtlety is what makes it complex, and because of that, this force requires a fair amount of planning. Although nudges must be well thought out, they're not nefarious or manipulative; they're done with positive outcomes for everyone in mind.

In *Nudge: Improving Decisions About Health, Wealth, and Happiness* (2009), authors Cass Sunstein and Richard Thaler explore the reasons why a subtle influence is so important. They write, "To put it simply, forcing people to choose is not always wise, and remaining neutral is not always possible" (p. 243). Consider parenting, for instance. Often as our children age, direct advice isn't heard, and a push or shove leads to alienation. Although a pull would be nice, if our relationship with a child is strained or we feel that a pull would prove too intense, a well-placed nudge can be precisely what the relationship requires. Whether through the use of some targeted questioning, a resource or book, or a modeled practice that may help a child learn an important lesson (without us hovering over the child or telling him or her what to do; we all know how challenging that can be), subtlety can leave a child's pride intact and a parent's stress at normal levels (for the moment, anyway).

We see the value of the nudge in our work lives as well. Imagine you're an instructional coach new to a building. You haven't formed a relationship with the building principal yet, and you have some thoughts about instructional practices that you'd like to see changed. A push or shove certainly won't work; you haven't yet built up a strong enough base to openly exert any influence. Plus, when was the last time you saw a building principal effectively shoved by a member of the staff?

What if, as an introduction to your great suggestions, you dropped off an article from *Educational Leadership* that explores one of the strategies that builds capacity in cross-subject literacy, something you think the school needs to put into practice? What if the article included a short note from you that explained how excited you were about the ideas discussed and that you think the practices fit the school really well? And what if you offered to discuss this with your principal, if there was the interest? In this case, you haven't applied any explicit force to the decision-making process. But what you *have* done (hopefully) is planted a seed for change, and although your principal may not pick up on it, you've left that seed out there to germinate. Time will tell whether the changes you think are necessary are made clear to your principal.

Your moves are in essence a nudge—a subtle, low-key, balanced use of influence that may (or may not) lead people to change their practice. Think of it like a light touch, a gentle breeze, a background noise.

Educators are well equipped to nudge. We do this as part of our daily work. High-efficacy teachers exhibit strong levels of planning and preparation, are persistent and resilient, and are willing to experiment with new methods (Brinson & Steiner, 2007). These attributes play a vital role in building a successful nudge. Consider the sentiment expressed by a teacher in a study (Henson, 2001): "If I try really hard, I can get through to even the most difficult or unmotivated students" (p. 5). Educators know they can influence students to engage and do their best without a push or shove, which are too direct to garner respect and change. If we can adapt the nudge to gently sway students, we can easily apply it to adults.

The When

When should we use a nudge? There are several instances that call for the use of this force.

When Positional Power Is at Play

Many of our relationships are driven by power exchanges. Even when used for good, power differentials affect our ability to get things done. But we can take the overt power dynamic out of the process. Nudges force a level playing field because the person driving change never has to claim taking action, and the person they're influencing retains the ultimate decision-making ability. Positions become momentarily meaningless because outwardly, nothing has happened.

When Relationships Need More Time to Consolidate

Relationships take time to form, and research shows that they should never be rushed; emotions play a fundamental role in reasoning and decision making (Immordino-Yang & Damasio, 2007). As educators, we know that student effort and engagement are directly related to the relationship that students have with their teachers (Osterman, 2000). Because leveraging positive relationships is the only effective way to accomplish anything well, we should use nudges when we're still getting to know people; we likely have a strong base relationship started, but we don't yet know each other well enough to use other forces. Networking experts agree that proceeding without getting buy-in is a mishap that can seriously undermine one's reputation. Nudging, however, can be done even when the relationship buy-in isn't yet firmly in place (Brustein, 2015).

There's another factor at work here, too. Sometimes because of the nature of the decision at hand, using any other force would potentially affect a relationship too negatively. This leaves us with no other choice than to nudge (or to do nothing at all, which is rarely a good option). The fact is, if we're worried about the future of a relationship and we can live with a hidden leveraging move, then applying subtle influence enables us to take a minimal risk with the potential for a large (or small) gain.

When You Can Afford to Fail

Whether you see a FAIL as the First Attempt In Learning or as something else entirely, failing at something can later help us excel. Failure can teach us where we went wrong in the first place and how we can learn to pick ourselves up again to succeed. Too often, people keep trying the same solution and keep getting the same result. Failure can teach us that it's not that we're bad at something; it's just that we have to try a different method to find success (DeWitt, 2012). Nudges are good if failure is an option.

Sometimes a situation requires a positive outcome, and anything else can't be tolerated. This may be our last shot to make a difference, and we have to make a difference *now*. For example, in attempting to form a new relationship with a professional learning organization, Fred and his colleagues realized that the design of the learning session should not be a hands-off experience. Rather than provide a nudge in hopes that the new partner would create a learning opportunity that would work for the region, the group had to work collaboratively through a pull to make the session a success. Leaving the design too much to chance could have negatively affected the future of the partnership.

Nudges are not good in these situations and should not be used if failure is not an option. Because a nudge is subtle, nuanced, and can take time to work, it's too risky a tool to use when immediate action is required. This also speaks to the fact that strategic planning is required to influence others in such a subtle way. You can't put out a fire with a nudge. You might only make it worse.

Let's now explore the positive and negative qualities of this force, which, of course, are always relative. Negative qualities may have no consequences in some instances, and positive qualities may result in little to no benefit in other instances. As we've found, every situation of leveraging relationships can differ.

- **The positives:**
  - Nudges have a low risk of retribution or blowback for the nudger.
  - Titles, positions, or power don't matter; anyone can nudge.
  - Successful nudges require strategic planning, always an important skill to hone.
  - Because of their subtle nature, nudges are unlikely to damage relationships.
  - There's no responsibility on the influencer to provide ongoing support.

- **The negatives:**
  - Nudges are subtle enough to be missed. There's no guarantee of success or even of catching someone's attention as a result of a nudge.
  - A lack of positional power means that action isn't mandated. You have to be comfortable knowing that nothing might change.
  - High initial involvement is required. Nudges take work, planning, research, and initiative.
  - Because of the subtlety of this force, nudges are unlikely to grow relationships.
  - When successful, little or no attribution is given to the person driving change.

As we read the following vignette, let's keep in mind the positives and negatives of nudge use.

A Voice from the Field

I often talk about writing articles and books with one of my colleagues who's also a close friend because it's of interest to us both. In one of our many conversations, I expressed my appreciation for professional organizations that have allowed me space to host my writing, enabling me to share my experiences with fellow educators.

Before submitting articles for possible publication, I often asked my friend to read the drafts and offer suggestions as a tactic to get her thinking about her own writing. Since then, we've had numerous conversations about her joining the writing world. She has deep knowledge in child development and learning needs; sharing her expertise in these fields would truly benefit educators.

So when a request for article submissions was posted about coteaching, I nudged her to go for it by sending her the request. She decided to write her first article draft, both of us hoping that this might be her first published article. This was an opening for her to also challenge herself professionally and take the next step in becoming an even greater asset to the professional community.

—Tamera Musiowsky
Former classroom teacher, ISS International School
Singapore

Musiowsky's experience provides valuable insight into the working of nudges. It's possible to begin nudging those around us when we share insights or personal reflection, subtly providing social cues to drive our colleagues' behavior. Although taking some work on the front end, nudges do not generally require ongoing support and assistance. In this case, the ball is in the colleague's court to do the work of writing and submitting. Will Musiowsky be credited with this support? Possibly, but that certainly shouldn't be the aim. Instead, the objective is to help others shift practice without any attribution; it's simply for the good of the person, community, or organization.

The Why

Why are nudges one of the four key Forces of Influence? How do they relate to the other three forces? Figure 7.1 shows a Forces of Influence Leadership Matrix that we've fleshed out with some examples for easy comparison.

As the matrix shows, nudges allow for high initial investment and low follow-up support. The idea is to work really hard to lay the foundation for a change, and then let the chips fall where they may. We do this to support a change while, at the same time, valuing that we aren't the decision maker in this particular case. We also nudge because at least one of the forces has to require some subtlety. As you've no doubt noticed by now, it's hard to hide a push, pull, or shove. Once they're used, it's easy for anyone to tell. Nudges occur at a safe distance, which makes them ideal in certain situations.

There's another important "why" here. Sometimes we want to adjust or course-correct without derailing overall good work or a positive direction.

Figure 7.1 **Sample Forces of Influence Leadership Matrix**

Much Ongoing Support

PUSH

Having a student teacher doesn't require much preparation, but the ongoing work is plentiful. New teachers need constant support and feedback to be successful. They're often nervous to take the reins in the classroom, and they require a little push to feel comfortable initiating lessons, maintaining control, and developing into the classroom teacher.

PULL

At our districtwide professional development day, instructional coaches ask district teachers to join them in presenting. Teachers often have a little trepidation and have to be talked into doing this. Coaches provide support by writing the professional development and suggesting facilitation tips before the presentation. They also serve as copresenters during the actual professional development.

Low Initial Involvement ← → High Initial Involvement

SHOVE

Professional development opportunities are costly to schools in terms of money and time. To recoup the expense of sending someone to a conference, teachers are often tasked with presenting to the faculty on their return. Teachers can be told to attend specific conferences, with the understanding that their schools expect a return on investment.

NUDGE

Getting teachers to come on board with new strategies— such as exploring how to use student-created lapbooks— can be challenging. If a teacher is currently using this strategy, all it might take to get other teachers interested is to showcase the strategy in a hall display. Teachers may jump on board of their own volition, without ever having been pressured to take on this practice.

No Ongoing Support

In a school in which Meghan worked, there was tremendous turnaround resulting in unbelievable student success. It was hard to argue with any ideas from leadership when they had all proven so successful. Nevertheless, having yet another initiative added to teachers' very full plates began to feel overwhelming. A coach in the building decided to have teachers list all the initiatives they were expected to implement daily and weekly, from enacting curriculum to completing wall displays. She kept this compiled list in plain sight in the staff room where the leadership team would see it. It was a subtle way to acknowledge that yes, these things worked, but adding more to overflowing plates would be challenging. This also encouraged everyone to speak in terms of specifics. Instead of lamenting about feeling overwhelmed, teachers could point to limitations in the schedule or competing initiatives, building their capacity to respectfully challenge ideas.

When we want others to lead for themselves, sometimes a nudge is actually what's needed. Nudges don't always have to be about leading up; sometimes the "why" behind a nudge is to grow leadership across a community and culture. And because you can't really *tell* people to lead, a nudge encourages people to grow for themselves.

A final reason for us to employ nudges in our practice? They build our capacity to be better strategic leaders and learners. As Peter Drucker may or may not have said, "Culture eats strategy for breakfast"; as our experience shows, strategy eats everything else for lunch, dinner, and dessert. In fact, strategy is so important to our growth as leaders that if we don't occasionally nudge others in our work, then we may never realize our full growth as a leader or the potential for leadership in others. If every leadership move we make is explicit, then we'll never be able to help others build the capacity for change on their own. Sure, a shove leaves change up to the person on the receiving end, but only after we've made it clear what changes need to be made. In a nudge, change is entirely up to the person receiving the nudge. This doesn't mean that we lead with *Game of Thrones*–style intrigue and deception. Rather, with the in-depth planning it takes to move others toward growth, we can truly see the value of strategy in our work. Nothing shows the benefit of strategic thinking like watching someone accomplish something that only you know you had a hand in jump-starting.

The How

Although there's always a risk of a nudge being unnoticed or intentionally ignored, there's a continuum of nudging strategies from least to more forceful. How you employ these strategies can also affect how they're received. For example, you might forward a link to an article to a broad audience you normally engage with that includes the colleague you'd like to influence. Or you might place a physical copy of an article in that person's inbox. A slightly more forceful approach is to write a note along with the article, highlighting the connection you hope the colleague will make in his or her reading. An even more personal route might be to hand the person the article while engaging him or her in a discussion about it. Each step is slightly more forceful and can elicit a different response. You can use a variety of levels in a nudge, depending on the time and effort you want to invest and how directly you wish to be tied to the potential outcome. Likewise, a nudge can become a push, pull, or shove when used in a more forceful way.

Nudging as a Continuum

Figure 7.2 outlines five nudges related to learning that move from subtle to more direct. As you read them, consider how you might put each level of nudging into practice in your work.

Figure 7.2 **Levels of "Nudginess"**

Higher level of nudginess	**See it/model it:** Although this is definitely more "nudgey," getting someone to observe a practice in action or modeling it for someone can be precisely what is needed to move a person in a new direction. You might try this: "Hey, there's an edcamp next Saturday one town over. Any chance you want to join me to check it out for an hour or two? I think it might be cool to bring that into our district." Remember that nudges are never forcefully explicit, so although a nudger can show something or model how a strategy could play out, a nudger isn't a pusher or shover at that same moment. Getting the person you want to influence to take action isn't forced.
	Article drop: It's hard to argue with evidence and easy to argue with opinion. One way to help nudge is to share an interesting article, research journal item, or document with your nudgee. It's a great way to get people to rethink their practices. For example, you might say, "I just wanted to pass this article on to you about personalizing professional learning. I thought it was interesting, and I wonder if it would help our staff as we start working on our PD initiatives for this year. I'd be happy to chat about it if you're interested."
	"I wonder" statements: Using these statements can be a well-veiled nudge. And using them is fairly easy. Instead of saying, "Could we have separate professional development sessions for teachers with different roles?" or even more direct, "Why can't we have separate professional learning sessions for those with different roles?" try something like this: "I wonder how the outcomes from this session would differ if there were separate sessions for those with different roles." By simply adding "I wonder" in front of a question, it puts the pressure on the asker, rather than on the answerer, while still giving the other person pause to consider.
	Collegial conversation: Collegial conversations happen continually, and the information shared in those conversations can provide insight for those around you. Likely, many nudges have come from conversations among colleagues. Strategically infusing your conversation with references to specific programs, methods, or practices can lead to an intentional nudge and one that is likely to stick, thanks to our inherent reliance on colleagues as a source of valuable information. You can make this strategy even less "nudgey" by waiting for the conversation to lead naturally to the desired topic instead of putting it out there yourself.
Lower level of nudginess	**Self-reflection:** Self-reflection is never intended to be a nudge, and yet our own practices can and do influence those around us. Simple conversations with others in which you self-reflect on what worked well, what didn't, and what you'll do differently in the future can influence others to not only examine their own actions, but also change their perspective or future actions.

The first rule of influence is taking the perspective of the colleagues you're trying to influence. Why is this issue important to them? How are they likely to act? What are the implications of not trying to influence them? Next, consider what you can do to remove obstacles that keep people from seeing the need for change. Can you leverage your relationship with others to help in this matter?

Although it might sound silly, writing down the nudge as you consider it might be just what you need to take action to make it happen. Putting the desired solution in a straightforward and succinct statement initiates a powerful ask of yourself. If the goal is large, consider breaking down obstacles into smaller goals. Finally, state your "if . . . then." For example, "*If* we update the type of professional development offered, *then* teachers will be more active participants and put training into practice."

As your nudges get stronger, consider adding a "because" to your if/then statements. This is the evidence you'll need to validate the success of the nudge. Did the outcome arise because of your nudging skill or simply because the time was right to reach the outcome? This is an important distinction. For example, "*If* we update the type of professional development offered, *then* teachers will be more active participants and put training into practice *because* they're well trained and supported and they see the value in change." Exit tickets and follow-up surveys or interviews would be a good way to measure this outcome.

Resources are important to any plan; determining what is and isn't at your disposal can help secure support for any initiative. Consider tangible resources such as classroom space or funding, intangible resources such as time and buy-in, and human capital. Do you have trainers and staff available, or will you need to seek them out?

Can you find available space in your building, or will you need to identify an available location somewhere else? The more resources you can identify and plan for ahead of time, the easier you make it for others to agree to your ideas.

Influencers and allies are perhaps the most valuable part of your plan. Are there people who will nudge with you? Are there people willing to support your ideas over the long term? Can you trust anyone to know that you're trying to exert subtle influence strategically, or are you going it alone? At what point do you want and need to let these influencers in on your plan? These are all important considerations when preparing to nudge.

Another consideration: who does the person you want to influence listen to? People are beholden to two groups—those they *must* listen to (the school community council, leadership teams) and those they *choose* to listen to (friends, valued coworkers). If you can boldly enlist the help of the latter outright, all the better. Otherwise, you might consider nudging them as well.

The Importance of Strategy

With the data in hand about influencers and allies, and given what you know about those you hope to influence, it's now time to select strategies. Will your colleague respond best to research-based articles or blogs featuring personal practice? What impresses the colleague more—what happens in high-performing schools in other states or local practices within his or her own school or district? Knowing the kinds of information and influences the person values will help you design your strategy.

Take time to plan by breaking down the overall goal into manageable pieces. The Nudge Action Template shown in Figure 7.3

Figure 7.3 **Nudge Action Template**

Challenge: The problem or challenge you want to solve
Desired Change: The resolution you desire
Impact (if/then): Your change written as an if/then statement: "*If* we do XYZ, *then* ___ will be the positive impact."

Resources: May be tangible (space, money); intangible (time, buy-in); or human capital (trainers, staff)

Resource Needed	How Resource Can Be Obtained

Resource Available	Role or Benefit

Influencers and Allies

Whom Do I Need to Influence?	To Whom/What Does He or She Listen?	Potential Nudge Strategies
Consider who the gatekeeper is, the decision maker. Who gives approval, or whom do you need to buy in?	Is the gatekeeper beholden to a certain group? Does the gatekeeper have personal or professional advisors?	Which strategies work best for the gatekeeper and his or her influencers?

Action Timeline

Action	Time Frame	Person Responsible
The specific activity you need to move toward your solution. Consider listing the actions in chronological order, from getting approval through carrying out the plan.	When will you work on or complete the action?	Consider your allies and committees.

can help with this work. What will you do first and when? Will you be the person responsible, or does the success of your actions rely on someone else? Envision the specific steps you need to reach your outcome—not only what you'll do before and during the nudge, but also what you'll need to do afterward to achieve your plan.

Benjamin Franklin may have said, "If you fail to plan, you are planning to fail." Now whether he did or didn't say it, experience shows us that this thought is certainly true for nudges. As far as Forces of Influence go, an unplanned nudge is a lost one. Only through well-thought-out strategizing can a nudge truly accomplish a goal.

As with all nudges, the end result is never known and is certainly never guaranteed. When any of us embark on a nudge, we do so with the understanding that its subtlety is both its strength and weakness. As we engage in situations that might not necessarily be ours to define, we do so with the lightest of touches and with only the slightest amount of acknowledged influence. Of course, as any good pebble can tell you, it only takes a light touch and a little momentum to create a boulder. We nudge for possibility and potential. It's truly a force that's meant to not be forceful in the end.

Roles and Relationships Check-In

We ask you once again to refer back to the Roles and Relationships Self-Assessment (see Figure 3.2, p. 52). Do any of your actions sound like a nudge? Are there instances where you used a different force but where a nudge might have been more effective? What small changes would you need to have made to create a nudge? Have you implemented nudges before that were ineffective? Now that you've read through all four forces, complete Part II of the assessment by listing the accompanying force alongside each role and set of actions you wrote down.

As we've noted, nudges don't require ongoing support, and yet you might be nudging toward an action that *does* require your ongoing involvement. When that happens, it's time to consider stacking forces, something we'll explore in the next chapter.

Questions for Self-Reflection

- What kinds of nudges have you used in the past? Which have worked? Which have not?
- What are your struggle points around nudging? How can you use the information in this chapter to grow?
- How can you use the strategic nature of nudging to build your skills as a strategic planner and thinker?
- Which of the categories of nudge use are you most comfortable with? Which are a constant struggle for you? How do you build on your work in each of these categories?
- Which nudging strategy can you start using immediately? Which strategies do you need to use to strengthen your work as a leader and learner? What can you do right now to make yourself more effective at influencing others?

Questions for Group Discussion

- In our group, who tends to be a successful nudger? What enables that person to use this force so well?

- What skills and characteristics do we believe are most beneficial in becoming more effective at nudging? How can we build on those skills/characteristics?

- Reflect on Sunstein and Thaler's quote, "To put it simply, forcing people to choose is not always wise, and remaining neutral is not always possible." Do we agree? What does that mean for the nudge as a Force of Influence?

- How did the vignettes shared in this chapter shape our thinking about using nudges effectively? What seems workable? What doesn't?

8

Stacking the Forces

It's no secret that learning is highly complex. If it were simple, we wouldn't find stressed teachers in every school in the country continually reinventing ways to reach students. We wouldn't have to study, nor would we ever forget things. But as it is, learning—and changing as a result of that learning—isn't easy. Although there are some agreed-on steps to enacting change, there's no consensus concerning the steps that must occur for change to take place.

Let's look once again at the two theories of change we discussed back in Chapter 6: Guskey's model and Desimone's model. Figure 8.1 displays the differences between them graphically. To recap, Guskey (2002) theorizes that teachers receive information through professional development that results in a change in practice. Changing practice influences learning outcomes for students, which, in turn, influence teacher attitudes and beliefs in a feedback loop of sorts. In Guskey's model of teacher change, it's *how* a change affects learning that determines attitudes and beliefs. In contrast, Desimone (2009) asserts that professional learning changes attitudes and beliefs *before* a change in instruction occurs and improved student learning can take place.

Figure 8.1 **Two Theories of Change**

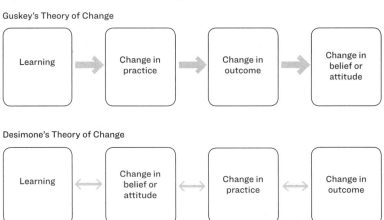

Sources: "Professional Development and Teacher Change," by T. R. Guskey, 2002, *Teachers and Teaching,* *8*(3), pp. 381–391; "Improving Impact Studies of Teachers' Professional Development: Toward Better Conceptualizations and Measures," by L. Desimone, 2009, *Educational Researcher, 38*(3), pp. 181–199.

If we hope to influence others, we have to believe our actions can change their actions. Does that mean we start by changing beliefs and attitudes? Or do we need to try an activity first? The theory of change you align yourself to might influence the force you're likely to pick. People who tend to use a push or a shove might believe that practice has to change before anything else can occur, so they may be more likely to get people started on an idea before anything else. People who usually pull or nudge might think changing attitudes and beliefs first is integral to effecting any sustainable change.

The windows of the Forces of Influence Leadership Matrix are large spaces with lots of flexibility. Because learning can be so complex, it might mean that we have to apply more than one force to create change. We may have to stack forces.

Fred first gained an inkling into the power of force stacking through an interaction he had with a colleague who was struggling to get a meeting off the ground. This person had some big challenges with the design of the session and came to Fred for assistance in planning. At first, Fred thought a push was necessary because of his colleague's relationship with those who would be at the session and the colleague's impressive wealth of knowledge. Fred suggested a few ideas and let his colleague know that he would be available to look over the created materials and provide feedback and assistance to help further shape the meeting.

Unfortunately for both of them, the push wasn't enough. The colleague was able to take a few steps forward but came back to see Fred later that day, somewhat distraught and far from comfortable with the design of the experience. Fred wondered how he might shift his approach to become truly helpful in this work. What would he do next?

It seems that Fred had misjudged his colleague's needs. Knowing that walking away wasn't an option and that his colleague needed this meeting to go well, he layered a pull on top of the push. Fred offered to help his colleague dive deeper into the design of the session, and he also offered to attend the session to provide feedback and insight. He saw his colleague relax and become more comfortable with the prospects of the work moving forward. Fred was able to provide design support, and he greatly enjoyed attending the meeting, which his colleague did a great job of facilitating.

The Importance of Context

Context is an important consideration in how learning will be perceived and implemented, in terms of environment—are we learning in a professional session or gleaning new ideas from a book we're reading at the beach?—as well as in role—are we a manager with the power to push or a new employee?

There are also discourse communities—the people we surround ourselves with—that contribute to our knowledge, views, and attitudes and that are paramount in shaping the way we view the world and our work (Putnam & Borko, 2000). Despite the best-planned and best-placed nudge, if the person we want to nudge is in a discourse community that's firmly against the suggested idea, we may not succeed. On the flip side, if our colleagues have all been trying out a new practice and then an article crosses our desk that supports that practice, we're far more likely to take note. Knowing the context of the person you wish to influence can help you understand how he or she might respond to a given force. But because there's no way to know or influence every aspect of context, it sometimes makes sense to combine or "stack" forces so you're sure to get your message across.

Every situation has different external factors that influence how well a force works, and not every situation can be perfectly planned for. Each force takes some forethought and practice to implement well. Appendix A, which you'll find at the end of this book, offers two role-plays to try in which you'll select a force and put it into action. You'll see that some forces might work better than others, but you'll also experience how each situation is unique. Try them out. What feels comfortable? What doesn't? When do you find yourself switching things up and stacking forces mid-scenario?

The Rationale Behind Stacking Forces

Stacking forces helps us layer strategies to effect change. When one force doesn't result in change or doesn't result in change fast enough, then an additional one might be necessary. We can't undo the first one. For better or worse, it's already out in the world. Stacking lets us mirror the complexity of learning and take a different approach. We aren't totally tossing out the baby with the bathwater; there are aspects of the first approach that remain no matter what we do.

When was the last time you had a Big Mac? Whether you're a fan of the fast-food staple or averse to anything from a drive-thru restaurant, we can't argue that the brothers McDonald understood the power of layering. One of the Big Mac's signature moves was the infusion of a second bottom bun that separated what was, in effect, one burger on top of another (the special sauce is pretty special, too). As if to say that sometimes one burger simply isn't enough, the Big Mac provided double the flavor and fun (and, if we're being honest, double the fat as well) by doing everything in layers.

And so it goes with force stacking. When one force is a poor fit or an insufficient effort to get the job done, we can build another one on top of it. We can't always plan this move in advance. It comes into play when goals aren't met, and it pushes us to be flexible enough to shift course to deploy another force to achieve our goal.

Stacking forces requires a good bit of time and effort. It makes the most sense to use this approach in situations that can't be abandoned or where a chosen goal must be met. This added strain on a relationship also means you should only stack your efforts when the relationships can handle it. You wouldn't (or maybe you *shouldn't*) eat a Big Mac if your stomach can't take it.

Keep in mind that intensifying your efforts isn't the only answer. Sometimes you will need to step away and admit failure rather than try to compel a change that isn't fully baked. But if you've made the decision to stack forces, it's a good idea to consider how to combine efforts that work well together. Although all the forces have merit, some pair up better than others. Pizza is good. Gelato is good. Gelato *on* pepperoni pizza is a recipe for a stomachache, whereas gelato *after* pizza might be just dandy.

To understand how you might approach force stacking, look back at the Forces of Influence Leadership Matrix (p. 45). Consider how strongly you have put yourself into any one quadrant. The closer you are to the middle of the matrix, the more likely you can make a small shift in tactics to a different strategy. The further from center you find yourself, the less likely you are to layer successfully. You might have to make a clean break and reenter with a different force at a later time, or you might have to switch gears entirely. This is not only jolting for you, but it also can be confusing to the person you want to influence.

Forces that are adjacent to each other tend to stack best because they have at least one aspect of the matrix in common. Diagonal forces are essentially opposites, and although they can be used in succession, they aren't a true "stacking" of forces. Figure 8.2 offers a series of possible stacking combinations.

A note about nudges. Nudges done right are very subtle, so they can potentially pair with any other force when implemented first.

Figure 8.2 **Stacking Forces—And Their Possible Combinations**

Force 1	Force 2	Stacking Considerations	Situation
Push	Pull	Pushes start with little initial involvement but a higher level of ongoing commitment. If the initial push doesn't result in change, think about following up with a pull. Backing up and getting more information might move the needle.	*I had a great experience with a novel last year that I was hoping my grade level would try out. I threw out ideas and wanted my coworkers to jump in, and I even offered to support them throughout the project. But they just couldn't envision it. So I offered to work on it with them, using the project from last year as an example. As a result, we successfully built a new project together.*
Pull	Push	Sometimes too much information can overwhelm those we pull. Backing off and letting them take the reins with a push can be an important part of getting them to take ownership.	*Being tech-savvy, I researched different apps our students could use when we went 1:1. I tried talking them up to get everyone excited, but they gave me the deer-in-the-headlights stare. Instead of pulling them into my world, I decided to challenge them to find an app they wanted to use on their own. Releasing control and putting the work on them was just the push they needed to get started, without me overwhelming them with information. They also knew I was just a step away, which helped them take risks.*
Pull	Nudge	Both pulls and nudges require some background work. A pull becomes a nudge when the level of ongoing commitment dwindles because the situation demands it. The less ongoing commitment the puller advertised from the start, the easier it is to layer on a nudge.	*Parents at our school wanted a student government association (SGA), and the PTA was vocal about creating one. The parents volunteered to run elections and meetings. One of the school's main concerns was that the parents were too involved and that students wouldn't be leading. So we decided, as a school, to work with the parents on creating the SGA together. Once it was designed, we took a backseat and let the parents experiment with some design elements. They subsequently proposed to help in the administrative tasks of setting up the SGA but added that they wouldn't attend meetings or control the direction of the group. Meanwhile, they continued to research how other schools set up their organizations.*

(continued)

Figure 8.2 *continued*

Force 1	Force 2	Stacking Considerations	Situation
Nudge	Pull	Nudges require having some background or research ready at the start, but once the nudge is applied, the nudger steps back and lets the result play out. If this feels too subtle or nothing is happening, the nudger might decide to add more ongoing support to move the action along.	*To get a youth engineering project going, I started sharing articles and program information about the value of STEM with my administrator. He signed up for the information sessions provided by the district, but the project didn't materialize. I eventually started asking about the program outright and volunteered to be a club coordinator or help others run the club to make it a reality.*
Push	Shove	A push is a commitment to ongoing involvement, but when even the promise of side-by-side help doesn't prompt action, sometimes it becomes necessary for a push to become a shove.	*Our school coach volunteered to help us acclimate to a new series of rubrics connected to a program we were taking on. There was little interest. Eventually, the coach and administrator insisted that we use the new rubrics. Those who didn't accept help were responsible for implementing them on their own.*
Shove	Push	In a successful shove, the person on the receiving end must take whatever action the shover deems necessary. But sometimes the process doesn't stop there. A successful shove may leave a shovee in a wholly new environment. With the requirement met, the shover may then take on a more supportive role.	*I put my teachers in charge of developing a schoolwide equity plan that would incorporate our new social-emotional learning curriculum materials. And develop it they did. The plan was well designed, practical, and filled with voices from school community members. The next big step was rolling this work out across the building. I let them know that I was here to support them as they engaged in this challenging process.*
Nudge	Shove	A nudge is used to make nuanced overtures toward a desired end. When the nudger is in a position of authority or is put in charge of a situation, he or she might turn to a shove if subtleties don't work.	*I tried to allow teachers to lead their own math professional learning communities (PLCs), with only very subtle involvement on my part. Despite my suggestions and the research data I offered, the discussions remained surface-level. The PLCs went in circles without accomplishing anything. I finally insisted that the teachers use specific protocol documents. Because I had laid some of the groundwork, I was able to get results when I finally put my foot down and demanded a change.*

Some Tips to Start Stacking

Layering strategies to influence others takes work. That said, here are some tips to help you along the way.

Recognize When a Goal Must Be Met or a Situation Can't Be Walked Away From

There are many times when it seems easier (and better) to throw up our hands and walk away from a situation. But this isn't always easy. That said, ask yourself if the goal you've set has to be achieved or if the situation is so important that failure is not an option. If either of these is the case, then you should probably layer your efforts.

Consider the Complexity of the Situation

The more complex a situation is, the more likely we'll need to incorporate more than one strategy to solve it. The stakes vary as well. Although some instances involve nothing more than giving someone a boost to take his or her classroom management practices from good to great, at other urgent times we must change the practices of others for the well-being of students and the growth of adults.

In her coaching role, Meghan works with teams during collaborative meetings. During one team meeting, she wanted to incorporate protocols to make the meeting run more smoothly and focus on student work. She thought a simple nudge would be enough. She brought copies of the protocol and said they were an option some other teams used. The team chose not to implement the protocols, and meetings deteriorated further. Meghan realized that there were compounding issues. The teachers didn't have a lot of trust in one another, they often felt pressure from administrators to adopt new practices, and Meghan didn't serve in an evaluative role.

To make the protocols a part of the collaborative meetings, Meghan had to stack a pull on top of her original nudge. She e-mailed the teams ahead of time with useful protocols, provided the forms during the meeting, and had team members practice using the protocols during the meeting. It took more than one force to resolve this complex situation.

Account for the Personalities Involved

The more people who are part of a given interaction, the more challenging it will be to bring the situation to a successful completion. Knowing that different personalities require different support methods, you'll probably have to layer your efforts to influence everyone involved. A few years ago, Fred and some colleagues found themselves writing a grant for a significant amount of state money. Their varied viewpoints seemed to be preventing any one force from working well. So on top of the original pull that had been used by Fred's supervisor at the time to start the work, a series of pushes were initiated to separate out the roles and work, creating a more effective process (and happily, their grant application was accepted for funding).

Consider What Combination Might Be Most Effective

Because layering relies on some common characteristic to work, combine your efforts with those similarities in mind to protect your relationships. For example, the common characteristic might be the certitude on the part of the person being influenced that ongoing support will be provided throughout. Relationships are delicate, and even in a worst-case scenario, we must do everything in our power to support those we serve. By using more than one strategy, we can sometimes reposition people enough to get them to where they need to be, and we can do so without leaving others high and dry.

Take Your Time

Stacking forces to influence others is not for the faint of heart. It means we have to be comfortable enough with ourselves to pivot, and it requires us to have built up enough trust, respect, collaboration, and listening power so that those with whom we're interacting don't get up and walk away in a difficult moment. When Fred and his colleagues were working on that grant, he invested a lot of time and energy into helping the group figure out the best ways to move forward. If it were not for the relationship capital he had previously built up, the situation would not have ended as well.

What does this process look like from soup to nuts? A variety of detailed stacking strategies are demonstrated in the flowcharts shown in Appendix B, which you'll find at the end of this book.

Sometimes forces just plain fail. What happens then? In our last chapter, we take a look at the aftereffects of using the Forces of Influence and how you can regroup if you must and move forward.

Questions for Self-Reflection

- What recent situation were you involved in that might have called for multiple efforts? How did you react then? Knowing what you know now, would you have done something different?
- Consider situations and relationships you're working through now. When would you choose to stack forces? When would you avoid this?

Questions for Group Discussion

- What do we consider to be the most complex aspect of using combined forces? When would we do this? When would we decide not to?
- Combined efforts require us to layer one force on top of another. What concerns with this process do we have? How might we work as a group to address them?
- Putnam and Borko (2000) found that discourse communities, the individuals we surround ourselves with, contribute to our knowledge, views, and attitudes and are paramount in shaping the way we view the world and our work. How does this research agree or disagree with our own findings in our organization?

9

When Forces Succeed and Fail

Have you ever asked yourself why we drive on a parkway and park in a driveway? As George Carlin wondered aloud in one of his many bits poking fun at our use and misuse of language, this question points to something that isn't quite right, truly a head-scratcher. And so it is with the forces. We've certainly scratched our heads many times and asked ourselves why a force didn't work as we meant it to work. Like milk that has just spoiled, sometimes what seems fine on the surface has suddenly gone bad.

Before coming to a new district, Meghan became a certified trainer for a variety of technology integration courses and certifications. She could provide trainings that would earn state continuing education credits. In her new district, teachers were responsible for earning a certain number of education hours outside the contract day. Meanwhile, the entire district was moving toward 1:1 implementation (one device for every student).

It seemed perfect to Meghan that she could offer training on a relevant topic and provide teachers with the hours they needed to fulfill their contract obligations at no cost to the school and in the convenience of her own classroom. Meghan mentioned her trainer status when teachers brought up training needs during meetings. She forwarded information on state trainings to the instructional coach and principal. As the year wore on, no one asked for guidance or training, even though she knew they needed help in the very topics she could support. So she decided to be a little more direct with her suggestions.

Meghan wanted the principal to approve the training, so she e-mailed him. She said that she could train the teachers for free in her classroom, and in return, they would get the continuing education hours they needed for their contract. She shared the overview of the different courses she could offer and said she would follow up during 1:1 implementation on her own time with any teachers needing ongoing support. The response from the principal? "I don't want to overwhelm anyone, so I think we just need to hold off." It made no sense to Meghan. Who could turn down such a great offer? She tried to drag the administration into her plan and, in doing so, got a hard no.

When Good Forces Go Bad (and Vice Versa)

Forces tend to go bad for one of three reasons, which we'll explore below. And then we'll dive into ways to recover. This process shares certain parallels with the hero's journey, which is based on the work of mythology scholar Joseph Campbell (1949) and film writer Christopher Vogler (1992). Although we've taken some liberties with the steps (as you'll see later on in Figure 9.1), much of the journey holds true.

So now let's introduce Jo, whose journey is about to start.

Meet our hero, Jo . . .

Jo is a typical teacher—overworked, underpaid, and working hard for her students every day. Students in her class and school are not as successful with reading comprehension as she would like, and the complex, compounding issues as to why that's the case and how to fix the problem feel nearly insurmountable. This is how we meet our Average Jo at the start of her journey.

All heroes are called to adventure, and for Jo that means being called on to do something about this issue of comprehension. Heroes in education are like heroes in Campbell's and Vogler's work; on their journey, they learn from others. Although Campbell's and Vogler's heroes are likely to meet a single mentor, Jo can learn from a great variety of characters around her, from coworkers and administrators to parents and other local stakeholders. Jo may have education relationships that extend beyond the school, such as a professional learning community or education organization. These relationships can also help mentor Jo in her quest for reading comprehension glory. So now, fired up as many heroes are, Jo decides to use a Force of Influence and pull, push, shove, or nudge her coworkers and administrators into action.

Let's now look at three ways our forces can sour.

Right Situation, Wrong Strategy

Let's start with the easiest failure to explain. Sometimes we simply put up a dud. Everything about the situation tells us that we need to apply a certain strategy for all the reasons we've discussed. Unfortunately, we misjudge, and although the situation truly *is* ripe for change, we blow it and use a push when a pull would have been better. After we're done banging our heads against the wall, it pays to examine why this might have happened.

- **We misread where people are in their growth.** Sometimes we believe that people might be ready to work together on something, but guess what? They might not be ready to put themselves out there at all. Despite our best intentions, we've all been in situations in which we simply misread people's readiness to make change, and therefore we misused methods to help them get there. When Meghan was teaching 4th grade, she became really excited about a project for the first novel of the year. When teachers came back in the fall, she shared the project, materials, and ideas about how to take on a major novel study. Despite her support, the other teachers were quite happy with the way they'd previously taught the novel. In addition, they were already feeling overwhelmed as the school year started. It seemed to them that Meghan was adding pressure for no reason, and the pull failed.

- **We acted too quickly.** In our desire to continuously improve our profession and the community in which we learn and grow, we might have acted too fast and missed important information that could have helped us to better match a force with a situation. Recently, Fred was in such a rush to build a new partnership that he nudged colleagues to help move the partnership along at a quick clip. However, a slower approach with a pull would have enabled the partnership to mature more effectively and would have likely reduced the overall stress levels of everyone involved.

- **We botched the delivery.** Maybe our nudge wasn't subtle enough, or maybe our pull didn't feel enough like a pull. In both cases, the force might not have felt appropriate to those we were seeking to influence, and therefore it failed in its goal. In Meghan's case, even though she was willing to train teachers to better support the school's 1:1 implementation, the teachers experienced her requests like a massive shove into something they weren't ready to take on. Because of her exuberance, she had failed to consult with her team and get buy-in on the front end, so the attempt to work on something new came off way more forceful than intended.

In all these cases, we have some cleaning up to do. When the situation is primed to apply a force but we've chosen the wrong one, we need to course-correct. In some cases, layering our efforts may be all that's needed to change course and salvage great results.

Jo missteps . . .
All great heroes tend to make mistakes when first grabbing hold of their powers. Campbell and Vogler refer to this as *trials and failures*. We call it a *failing force*. Jo decides to push her teammates to start looking at reading comprehension solutions. She knows that her coworkers are concerned about

comprehension issues, but they can be slow to act. So she decides to take on the task of finding new material for them. She throws out the pacing guides and district curriculum, and tells everyone they're going to use the new and wonderful materials she just found online.

Jo starts using the wrong force for the right situation. In her rush to action, she simply doesn't consider how others would feel. Her coworkers think she's belittling their teaching. She didn't talk with an administrator before abandoning district resources, nor did she fully vet the new materials. Uh-oh, Jo.

Right Strategy, Wrong Time

Timing is truly everything. You wouldn't necessarily offer someone hot tea in the middle of a scorching summer, and you wouldn't (spoiler alert) reveal that Darth Vader is Luke's father to someone who hasn't yet seen the original *Star Wars* trilogy. There's truly a time for everything, including influence. In some cases, a push or a shove is necessary, but we apply it at times that don't make the most sense, and in so doing, we shift from success to failure. By acting at less-than-opportune times, we typically end up with less-than-opportune results.

By gaining experience in understanding when the time is right to use a force, we'll become more capable of using the right force at the right time. Here are three look-fors to help determine when the time is right.

- **The person you hope to influence recognizes that something is "off."** We've all had experiences in which we know something is wrong. We get that feeling in our gut that tells us that things are not as they should be, and depending on how we handle those stressors, either we're able to work through it on our own or we need the help of others. The key, of course, is recognizing that we have to do something (or something has to be done to us). When people acknowledge that things are not as they should be, it becomes easier to accept the fact that change is necessary. At that point, they become more open to support and influence.

• **You're striving for a community-wide capacity for the change.** Strategies to influence others can become "more right" when the culture and community see the change as being necessary or desired. When people are on board with a given change, the mutual accountability of taking on the hard work can be enough to help people lower their guard, buckle down, and adjust their practice. When we all see the value of something, we all become more inclined to take responsibility for it. By welcoming some of that responsibility, we welcome the fact that others may be able to help us adjust what we do and how we do it.

In the years directly after the 2008 recession, many educators recognized that changes to elements of contracts and working conditions were required. Little direction was needed from school district leaders because the community as a whole recognized that all were struggling. As of late, more energy and effort have needed to be put into forces applied around changes in working conditions; although the economy has strengthened, educator compensation has not followed suit. This reality, combined with local and national politics, helped teacher groups apply the Forces of Influence both to one another to organize and to their leaders to make changes to working conditions. The "Red for Ed" movement served as a time when the Forces of Influence could be utilized to reverse changes that stemmed from the recession of 2008.

- **A qualifying life event has taken place.** Although this might sound like an advertisement for a health care plan, sometimes shifts in our professional or personal lives provide us with exactly what we need to see why a new path must be forged. Whether it's a marriage, a new job, a birth, a never-expected opportunity, a death, or anything else that upends our normal routine, life's ebbs and flows can be precisely what we require to awaken our understanding of the need for something different.

Ten years ago, Fred never would have expected that his educational leadership work would take him to where he is today. Assuming a traditional pathway was in store, he was in the midst of applying for assistant principal positions when a regional opportunity became available, somewhat out of nowhere (at least, according to Fred). Pushed by some, and as he found out later, nudged by others, he took a risk and found himself in a totally new environment, one that was both a match for his skills and an amazing place to continue his learning and growth.

Jo gets her timing wrong . . .
Pushing teammates, regardless of their trusting relationship, wasn't the right thing for Jo to do. Now, the administration *is* truly worried about reading comprehension and is certainly open to exploring options. But changing up instruction

drastically in February, with all that entails for teachers, is a hard ask, even if Jo is willing to work alongside coaches and textbook selection committees. Teachers don't have the time to focus on and organize new materials. Many standards have already been taught; new material would change the scope and sequence of what is needed and when. The curriculum team won't convene until late April, after testing, to look at new materials. Jo might be on the right track with her pull, but her timing couldn't be worse.

Right Strategy, Wrong Person

Sometimes the strategy itself makes a ton of sense. For instance, maybe we're in a situation in which we don't have much positional authority, and it seems like nudging our supervisor is the right approach to help that person make a change in practice. As we've learned, though, using these strategies is as much about matching them to the person as it is about matching them to the situation. Even the best strategy will fall flat if the person isn't a match. That's why we have to know the person (or people) and ourselves—and know everything else (or as much as we can).

- **Know our people.** Knowing the people we learn and lead with is a necessity if we're to continuously grow (and help others do the same). By doing so, we can make sure that our force selections not only match a given situation, but also fit the people we're working with.
- **Know ourselves.** It's also important to understand a bit about ourselves. Sometimes, we aren't the right person to be applying the force for any number of reasons. Maybe we don't have the

best relationship with the person we're trying to influence. Or maybe we just don't have enough skill with the given strategy yet. In any event, to best influence others, we need to pay attention to ourselves. If our efforts fail, it's entirely possible that the reason might be us! It can be hard to implement a force, even something that has worked in other situations, when relationships are just getting off the ground. Meghan has come into coaching situations where relationships with past coaches were not strong. In those cases, if she wants to use a force, she's had to rebuild relationship trust and communication.

- **Know everything else.** Yes, this sets the bar extremely high. And no, there's no way we can ever know everything. This caution simply points to the fact that interactions are rarely just about the people directly affected. They're also about what's happening in the school or district that day, what was served for lunch (and when), and what the weather is like. All this is to say that sometimes forces land well (or don't) because people are in places they usually aren't. Sometimes failure is simply luck and circumstance.

Jo takes things from bad to worse . . .
Jo is struggling. While at the neighborhood ballpark, she chats with parents in the community and explains why a change in reading comprehension teaching is so vital to students. She thinks that if she can convince the parents, she'll be well on her way to shifting teaching at the school. One parent doesn't really know what Jo is talking about, but she politely listens and lends support. One parent thinks Jo is saying that the *parents* are responsible and that teachers are

blaming the students instead. One parent shares Jo's concerns but feels the time is wrong for the adoption of a new approach and new materials. And one parent ends up complaining to the school about the reading comprehension scores and blaming the *teachers* for those poor scores—not an outcome Jo wanted at all.

So Your Force Has Failed

So maybe it isn't your best moment. Maybe the strategy you applied didn't land so well. Maybe you failed so spectacularly that it is meme-worthy. Maybe, unlike in the *Star Wars* trilogy, using the Force didn't save the world (or help you learn you had a sister or were related to your archenemy, but we digress).

The good news? Failure is key to learning, and without regular failure, it's unlikely that we'd ever learn enough to truly get better. As Moroccan politician Lahcen Haddad (2018) said, "Failure is simply success suspended, until the time is right." When forces fail, we need to try, try again. And there are a number of ways we can do that. In the hero's journey, this is where our hero is on the rebound. No good hero stays down for long; the best heroes make amends and attack the problem from a different direction. Here's how you can do that.

- **Layer your strategies.** Just because one strategy doesn't get us there doesn't mean we have to stop. In many cases, a situation is intense enough to require more than one strategy. Layering strategies can turn a failure into a success and can remind us that few aspects of relationships and support are simple. Complex interactions often require complex solutions!

- **Do more research.** Any type of failure is often a signal that we need to collect more information. When a force fails, it makes perfect sense to take some time and learn more. Like an Everlasting Gobstopper, that fictional candy from Roald Dahl's *Charlie and the Chocolate Factory* that perpetually changes colors and flavors, there are always more layers to a situation than at first meet the eye. Taking a failure as a sign to dig deeper is a great way to use failure to our advantage.

- **Seek the shadows.** We're not talking about a horror flick here; we don't want you to lie in wait, then jump out and scare someone—just to make yourself feel a little better about failing. Rather, this is a reminder that we may need to step back and remove ourselves from the situation to better understand why we failed and what our next steps might be. Few situations require immediate action. If our first attempt didn't work, taking time to rethink our position and gain new perspective may be precisely what we need.

- **Find a buddy.** For most of this book, we've looked at strategies to influence others as a solo enterprise, as something *you* do, rather than something *we* can explore together. In some cases, seeking a buddy to help you strategize or analyze your current plans can get you closer to success. Buddy forces can be doubly powerful, but they also require double the coordination. Nevertheless, they can be useful to overcome challenges to using forces that we might not be able to overcome on our own.

- **Apologize.** Sometimes the path to recovering from a misguided attempt is simply to apologize to the person or people we attempted to influence. If those on the receiving end understand that what we attempted to do was for worthwhile reasons (our own growth, stronger outcomes for learners, a more developed community, and so on), then they will most likely view the apology as authentic and meaningful. Apologies are most powerful, of course, when they don't come all the time. That said, if we feel that a strategy didn't work because of an error we could have prevented or corrected, and we now worry that the relationship will be strained as a result, then a well-placed apology can go a long way.

Jo recovers . . .
Jo decides to implement a few of our rescue strategies. She apologizes to her teammates for making them feel as though the reading comprehension issues were their problem alone, and she lets her coach and administrator know she's back to the regularly scheduled curriculum. By finding a buddy in the reading coach and pulling each other along, Jo is able to work through some of the holes in the curriculum and improve her own practice. Before the curriculum team meets in April, she'll be able to show what research says about the most effective strategies for teaching reading comprehension, where the holes in the current program are, and how the school can best address students' needs in this area.

Let's recap how you, an unsuspecting superhero, might find yourself on what we call the Influencer's Journey (see Figure 9.1). You've no doubt already started building relationships, ones that may influence you or that you hope to influence as you notice the need for change. This need for change might be intrinsic or extrinsic, but either way, you're off on your journey. When you use these strategies to try to

Figure 9.1 **The Influencer's Journey**

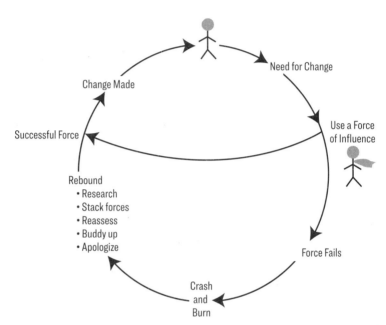

influence others, you step over into the realm of the unknown; there's no way to fully anticipate how a strategy will land.

For whatever reason, the strategy you use fails (the wrong time, wrong force, or wrong people), and you crash and burn. The good news is that you're like every other superhero, and guess what? The hero never dies! You use any number of rebounding strategies such as apologizing, teaming up with a buddy, reassessing and researching, or layering your force. You're ready to try again, and this time you're successful! Not only does your strategy have the intended outcome, but you also build relationships in the process. You really are quite the superhero (and now you can create your superhero costume for the next comic book convention).

Tying It All Together

It all comes back to relationships. We started this book with the idea that relationships are the foundation for all influence to occur. If we capitalize on the key components of collaboration, listening, respect, and trust and use them to foster positive interactions, we create an environment in which failure doesn't mean forever. The stronger the relationship, the more likely a misdirected strategy or a failure can be smoothed out. Just look at two recovery strategies—for example, seek a buddy and apologize. Both capitalize on relationships to repair damage and move forward.

In Campbell's and Vogler's work, the hero is often given a gift before returning to the mortal realm, where he or she is changed for the better. Maybe Jo gets to be on the curriculum team, is given funding for additional reading materials, or is able to attend additional training. But for our hero, there can be no better gift than building new relationships. Maybe Jo had a rocky path, but she was able to repair the relationship with her team and grow a deep professional bond with her coach. She has earned the respect of her administrator as someone who will thoughtfully approach a problem and guide others to a solution (or three).

So let's take a moment to reflect on what we've explored throughout this book, as well as on each of the forces and its use. As Cyril Houle, pioneer of adult education, is credited with saying, "If you teach a person what to learn, you are preparing that person for the past. If you teach a person how to learn, you are preparing them for the future." Metacognition, or self-awareness of one's own knowledge, is how we critically assess our own learning to maximize cognitive skill and learn from experiences. Consider keeping notes of how you are influencing others strategically throughout your work, not just at the end of it. It can be easier to document how your choices led to actions and to recall emotions in the moment rather than later on. That said, sometimes opportunities for influence present themselves, and we don't have the time to make in-the-moment reflections.

Therefore, let's do just that. Take a moment to consider your findings from your Roles and Relationships Self-Assessment from Chapter 3 (p. 52) that has helped you throughout this book identify the forces you use in your various roles. Here are some questions to consider:

- What strategy are you most likely to use? Is that a self-selected strategy, or do you feel pushed into using it? Why do you tend toward using that force?
- Are you surprised by your trends? What surprises you and why?
- What strategy are you not implementing? Why? What barriers are preventing you from using that force, and what potential positive outcomes could come from trying it?
- Are there similarities between the roles you take on and the methods you're most likely to implement?
- Now that you've reflected on the strategies you usually use and how each one has worked for you, which force are you more likely to try?

Force, Actions, Emotion, Reaction

Now let's take a deep dive to consider one specific situation you've had with using a force. It might be a force that worked well, didn't work at all, or required stacking. The following questioning process will help you reflect on forces as you use them:

- **Force:** Consider the strategy you used. Did you intentionally select that strategy, or did something drive you to that path that was outside your control? No matter what strategy you found yourself using, why did you end up there?

- **Actions:** Think through each step you took to implement the force, including actions you took alone. Maybe you researched potential solutions to a problem. Maybe you set up a meeting or made direct asks. Record each action (here's where recording throughout your process might help).

- **Emotion:** Try to identify how each action made you feel (which, in turn, likely drove your next actions). For example, you might have felt excited and prepared when conducting research. You might have felt anxious to make a direct ask and relieved when you got an answer.

- **Reaction:** People are rarely direct enough with their own emotions to tell you how your actions made them feel. Likely, you had to interpret how your actions affected others by considering their reactions. For each action you took, what was the resulting reaction? Look for moments when emotions seemed to change or you noticed others either endearing themselves to you or clearly deciding against your planned course of action. Think through each action you took and each emotion you experienced, and consider how those moments affected the lives of others. It's possible, and even likely, that you influenced more people than your intended target. Were coworkers, friends, or family drawn into your strategy by association? What reactions did they have at each step of the way?

We've put together the following Force-Actions-Emotion-Reaction questioning tool to help you reflect on forces as you use them:

- **Force:** What force did you select? Why?
- **Actions:** What specific actions did you take to implement the force?
- **Emotion:** For each action, how did you feel? What were your expectations and trepidations?
- **Reaction:** How was each action received? How did those you influenced react?

The End Is the Beginning

Over the course of this book, we've tried to set the context for incorporating the Forces of Influence into our lives. Relationships are the vehicle that help us do good work, and influence and leverage are the keys to move that vehicle along. Because almost all of our relationships are transactional in nature, we need to use leverage to get great things to happen.

To do so, we need to put a number of strategies into action. Each strategy is different and requires different situations, people, and moves to be successful. Sometimes one strategy isn't enough, and sometimes no amount of forces will ever lead to true success. In the end, the Forces of Influence present a toolkit to add to our shed of learning and leading moves. And like a great set of tools, we should always have them at the ready when we work with others to accomplish great things.

Questions for Self-Reflection
- How do you tend to approach failures in your life? What do you do to move past them?
- Which of the reasons for force failure discussed in this chapter can you relate to most? Why?
- Now that you've finished reading this book, where are you on your journey? Do you feel better prepared to use the forces? What questions are you still asking? What support do you still need?

Questions for Group Discussion
- How do we tend to react to failure in our organization? Is it considered good? Bad? Neither? Both?
- What options exist for us to continue to grow? How do we turn challenging situations into future successes?
- Over the course of this book, what has stuck out most for us? What do we agree with? Argue against? Aspire to?
- How might we use the Force-Actions-Emotion-Reaction questioning tool in our work when we reflect on force use?

Appendix A: Role-Play Scenarios

The two role-play scenarios that follow—one at the secondary level and the other at the elementary level—can be used in small- or large-group settings to try out different Forces of Influence. Role-play partners should take turns playing both the forcer (the person using a Force of Influence) and the forcee (the person the force will be used on). This will promote rich conversation and provide insight when similar situations arise in real life.

Note that force choices aren't so much right or wrong as they are better or worse suited to a given situation. Use what you've read to make informed decisions about the best forces to use and why they make the most sense.

Role-Play 1, Secondary Level: Selecting New Mathematics Resources

Forcer: Mathematics Teacher

You're a mathematics teacher in a hierarchical high school. Your department, under the direction of your department chair, has been tasked with selecting new mathematics resources for the following school year and determining the professional development needed to support those resources.

Despite the findings of the department that a move toward a more student-centered series of resources is the best choice, the department chair announces that a different series of resources will be selected. When prodded, the department chair states that the principal is concerned with matching the traditional resources used by the other high school in the district. There's concern that if a drastic resource shift is made (as the department is suggesting), student scores on state and local assessments may drop, leading to the perception that math teaching and learning at your high school is less effective. In addition, the principal is concerned about the varied professional development that a student-centered approach might require; teachers may need too many days out of the classroom for training, and the school might need to invest in too many experts to provide the continued growth.

Despite the anger and frustration experienced by the department, your chair says that "nothing can be done" and that "the decision has been made."

After the meeting, your departmental colleagues come to you. They know that you have extensive math experience, have taught in the district for many years, and are well respected by students and staff. They ask you to attempt to shift the thinking of your chair or principal (the two forcees listed below).

Questions for Discussion

After you've played the role of the forcer (the mathematics teacher) with each of the two forcees (the department chair and the principal), consider the following questions:

- What force did you use? Why?
- What additional information would have helped you use the force more successfully?
- What effect did the role of the person you were attempting to influence have on your choice of a force?

Forcee 1: Department Chair

When you share your decision to shift to more student-centered resources and individualized learning with your principal, she declines it. She says that scoring must be consistent across the district, and that although she appreciates your lobbying for the other resource set and personalized professional development, the decision has been made. You tell your department, letting them know that you tried but were overruled. Your department is angry, but you don't know what else you could do.

Forcee 2: Principal

As principal, you reject your department chair's suggestion to move to more student-centered resources in math and point to the personalized professional development that would be required as being far too time-consuming, given your overall lack of resources. Your central administration is concerned about scores and resources being similar across your two district high schools, and there's worry that a shift to a different model would negatively affect student results on local and state assessment measures, and therefore negatively affect community perspective. Although you value your math department and chair, you can't risk negative outcomes for students or teachers.

Role-Play 2, Elementary Level: Helping Out a New Principal

Forcer: Teacher

A good friend and colleague of yours has just been promoted from a teacher in your grade level to the school's new principal. One of his first actions in this new role is to lead a portion of the school's opening faculty meeting. Your colleague is nervous and knows that transitioning from one role to another in a school is challenging. He's well respected and was a strong teacher, but he's always sensed that a lack of self-confidence has held him back professionally.

He comes to you to ask for your help in putting his portion of the faculty meeting together. The transition has been hard for him, and he misses the planning and camaraderie that you shared for years. He makes it clear that his segment of the meeting needs to be seen as being developed by him, but he feels much more comfortable collaborating with you, his closest colleague, to put this type of learning together. He worries that if he went to the assistant superintendent or another member of the administrative staff, it would reflect poorly on his ability to be successful in this role from the start.

After listening to your colleague, you must decide how you will use a Force of Influence in this situation.

Questions for Discussion

After you've played the forcer (the teacher) with the forcee below (the new principal), answer the following questions:

- What force did you attempt to use? Why?
- What additional information, resources, or allies would have been helpful in using the force successfully?
- What effect did the role of the person you were attempting to influence have on your choice of a force?

Forcee: New Principal

You've just received a wonderful promotion to serve as a principal in a school you've worked in for close to two decades. Although you're nervous about leaving the classroom, you're excited about what this role might bring. There's a big challenge, though, right at the start. Within weeks of your promotion, you're being asked to lead a significant portion of the school's opening day faculty meeting. Although you've led meetings previously, most of them have been for the teachers in your grade level; you've never facilitated learning for over 50 people at a time, and the group you'll be addressing soon is far larger than that. The assistant superintendent, your mentor, has only been in the district for a year. Although she's nice, you haven't yet developed a strong enough relationship to ask her for her help.

Nervously, you approach your close colleague, who taught with you for most of your career. You recognize the challenge of asking for her help, but you also know that your future success depends on starting the year off well. You also believe that you need to take full credit for this work; you aren't looking for someone to do the work for you, but you *are* looking for someone to help guide you to put together what will make the most sense for the meeting.

Appendix B: Stacking Strategies Flowchart

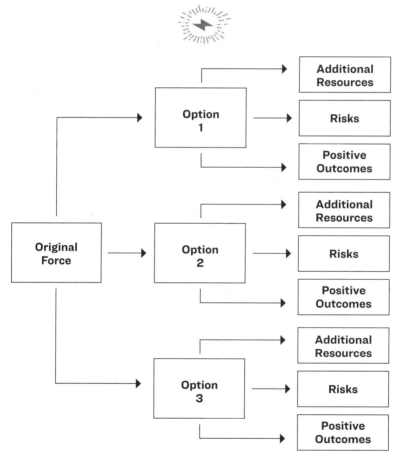

Note: The "original force" refers to the force you've selected to use. Options 1–3 refer to each of the remaining forces that you may choose to "stack" on top of the original force. For each pairing, we suggest additional resources that may be needed, risks you may run, and positive outcomes that may result. We also illustrate each pairing with an example from practice.

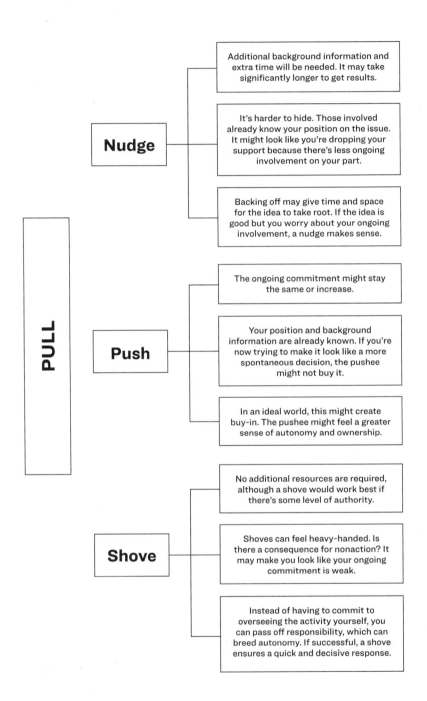

PULL

Nudge

Additional background information and extra time will be needed. It may take significantly longer to get results.

It's harder to hide. Those involved already know your position on the issue. It might look like you're dropping your support because there's less ongoing involvement on your part.

Backing off may give time and space for the idea to take root. If the idea is good but you worry about your ongoing involvement, a nudge makes sense.

Push

The ongoing commitment might stay the same or increase.

Your position and background information are already known. If you're now trying to make it look like a more spontaneous decision, the pushee might not buy it.

In an ideal world, this might create buy-in. The pushee might feel a greater sense of autonomy and ownership.

Shove

No additional resources are required, although a shove would work best if there's some level of authority.

Shoves can feel heavy-handed. Is there a consequence for nonaction? It may make you look like your ongoing commitment is weak.

Instead of having to commit to overseeing the activity yourself, you can pass off responsibility, which can breed autonomy. If successful, a shove ensures a quick and decisive response.

Pull

As the grade-level chair, I want to get my team to use practitioner inquiry. I've shared my ideas and shown my team members how it could work. I plan to work right alongside them while we tackle our problems of practice. They still aren't interested.

Nudge

I start a practitioner inquiry project of my own and share the information as I go along, but I don't actively try to get my team involved anymore.

- I'll have to find someone else willing to talk through my problem of practice with me if the team isn't going to do so. I'll still need to share my information as I go along.

- It's going to take a lot longer to get everyone on board, and I'm not even convinced that they think what I'm doing is valuable. They might think I'm being a show-off, doing it on my own without them.

- If the team members see that my inquiry has positive student outcomes, they might be more likely to try it. They might see what doing their own study could look like and the benefits that could result.

Push

I start a practitioner inquiry project of my own and bring my work to the PLCs. I ask for help from the team members and make them an integral part of the process.

- I would have to start my inquiry alone, but I've already given them the information I think is important.

- Team members will probably recognize that I'm going ahead without them and that I still want them to do the work. If the administration praises me, it might feel like I left them out.

- If the team members help me with my inquiry, they'll see how easy it can be to fit that inquiry into my current work. Because they're helping me, they're inherently part of the process.

Shove

Because I'm the grade-level chair, I could just tell everyone this is the process we're going to do for our PLCs. I could hand out forms and say they're due at the next meeting.

- I'd need to assemble any forms so my team members have a structure they'd have to stick to. I'd have to set deadlines and check on the work, along with setting all the meeting agendas.

- The team members might not be very happy with me saying that they have to do all the work. If they come to meetings without their work, it makes them look bad and they'll be mad at me.

- If they would just get started with the process, I think they'd really like it. If I force them into getting started, we could all be working on the same timeline and issues together.

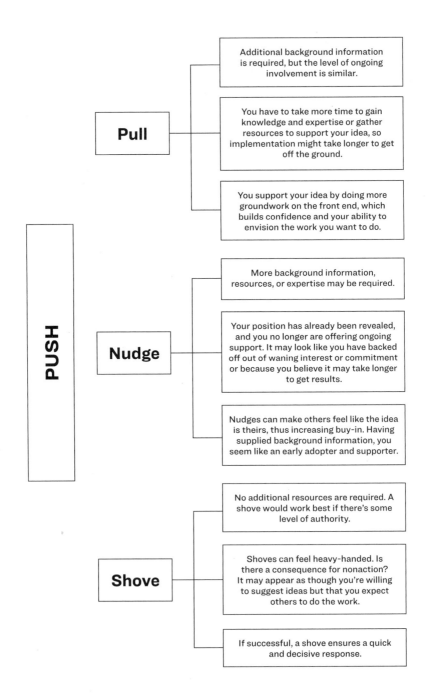

PUSH

Pull

Additional background information is required, but the level of ongoing involvement is similar.

You have to take more time to gain knowledge and expertise or gather resources to support your idea, so implementation might take longer to get off the ground.

You support your idea by doing more groundwork on the front end, which builds confidence and your ability to envision the work you want to do.

Nudge

More background information, resources, or expertise may be required.

Your position has already been revealed, and you no longer are offering ongoing support. It may look like you have backed off out of waning interest or commitment or because you believe it may take longer to get results.

Nudges can make others feel like the idea is theirs, thus increasing buy-in. Having supplied background information, you seem like an early adopter and supporter.

Shove

No additional resources are required. A shove would work best if there's some level of authority.

Shoves can feel heavy-handed. Is there a consequence for nonaction? It may appear as though you're willing to suggest ideas but that you expect others to do the work.

If successful, a shove ensures a quick and decisive response.

Pull

I pull together some information on planning, gather shared resources such as planning templates, and e-mail the team and coach with days and times they could meet. I volunteer to set aside faculty meeting time to learn about backward design.

I need to set aside time and space for teachers and the coach to work together, supporting them with planning documents or professional resources as needed. I'll need to check in on the team after planning to see how it went.

The team could still refuse to plan or could plan in a way that I feel is inappropriate. Team members might resent my ongoing involvement because they've had autonomy over their planning in the past.

The team and the coach work together to plan pacing and instructional delivery that support all learners. I'm appreciated for providing resources, time, and space to work.

Push

As principal, I want my teachers to do more intentional planning. Because lesson plans aren't required, I fear that teachers are winging it and that they would be more successful if they did some backward designing using common formative assessments and district pacing. In a team meeting, I told the team they should plan with the coach and that their time will be compensated. They still didn't do any planning.

Nudge

Realizing that my directness isn't working, I start to gather information and resources on planning for the team, but I give this material to all the teachers so no one feels called out. When planning upcoming professional learning, I make sure to have the coach model planning and backward design. Teams that do plan are highlighted in our weekly staff celebrations.

I have to pull background information and plan learning experiences for teachers that highlight the practices I want them to use.

Team members could feel that they've gotten away with not planning and that I've backed off my idea. They might feel undersupported, or they might not realize that the professional learning and celebrations are intended for their ears.

My teachers will realize that planning is a best practice, and they'll feel supported with the professional resources provided. Because they come to the conclusion themselves, I don't look like I'm taking away their autonomy.

Shove

I tell teachers that they will be planning with the coach and that I expect to see lesson plans starting next week.

I don't have to collect or share resources. I only need to ensure the plans are completed by my deadline.

I come across as authoritative and could risk some relationships. My teachers don't feel supported because I didn't offer help, time, or resources. Plans aren't done my way because I didn't specify a format.

Teachers begin planning with the coach immediately and are clear on my planning expectation.

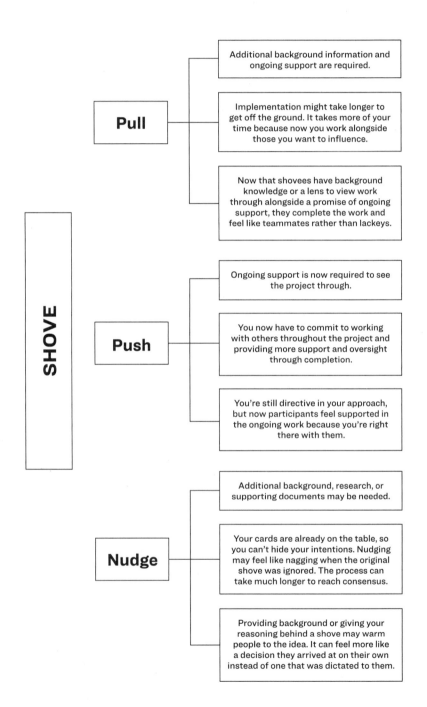

SHOVE

Pull

- Additional background information and ongoing support are required.

- Implementation might take longer to get off the ground. It takes more of your time because now you work alongside those you want to influence.

- Now that shovees have background knowledge or a lens to view work through alongside a promise of ongoing support, they complete the work and feel like teammates rather than lackeys.

Push

- Ongoing support is now required to see the project through.

- You now have to commit to working with others throughout the project and providing more support and oversight through completion.

- You're still directive in your approach, but now participants feel supported in the ongoing work because you're right there with them.

Nudge

- Additional background, research, or supporting documents may be needed.

- Your cards are already on the table, so you can't hide your intentions. Nudging may feel like nagging when the original shove was ignored. The process can take much longer to reach consensus.

- Providing background or giving your reasoning behind a shove may warm people to the idea. It can feel more like a decision they arrived at on their own instead of one that was dictated to them.

Shove

The district has adopted a new science curriculum. As the science coordinator, I deliver the message to principals and teachers that they will be using the new curriculum in the fall. Although the materials have already been purchased and delivered, I'm afraid that implementation will be spotty and that the intention of the program will be lost. Or the teachers may even ignore it altogether in favor of how they've always taught.

Pull

Realizing that teachers need much more support to understand the program as well as the ongoing professional learning required to implement it, I work with my coaches to develop districtwide professional learning and coaching plans.

- I help coaches build and deliver professional learning before the summer starts, so teachers can understand the program layout. Ongoing professional learning on program implementation, planning, and delivery supports are all put in place with our coaching team.

- It's still possible that teachers will revert to their old ways of teaching using old materials. I have a much greater time and effort commitment to seeing that implementation is done effectively.

- Because teachers were given time to understand the reasons we chose the program and how the program is structured, and because they received ongoing support, they implement the program with fidelity and achieve better student outcomes. This isn't something the district did *to* them but *for* them.

Push

I'm not going to justify how and why we selected the program, but I will make sure that coaches are in schools providing ongoing planning and implementation support on site across the district.

- I need to make sure coaches are available and offer ongoing modeling, coteaching, and planning support for teachers.

- Teachers will not get the background of the program or understand why we're implementing this new way of teaching. Without that, they might not see the reason to comply with implementation at all.

- Having on-site coaches who can help when needs arise ensures that teachers are supported throughout the year as they try the new program.

Nudge

Teachers might not understand what makes the new program so different and why implementation should be carried out in a certain way. I'll set up optional professional learning opportunities for teachers before the school year starts and make supporting documents available on the district website.

- I have to create learning opportunities to give teachers background on the curriculum layout, design, and selection process, along with documents they can access online.

- Not applying ongoing support might limit the amount of implementation that happens. Optional professional learning and online resources aren't direct enough to garner much traction.

- Teachers appreciate the available resources and don't feel as though they're being watched over throughout implementation.

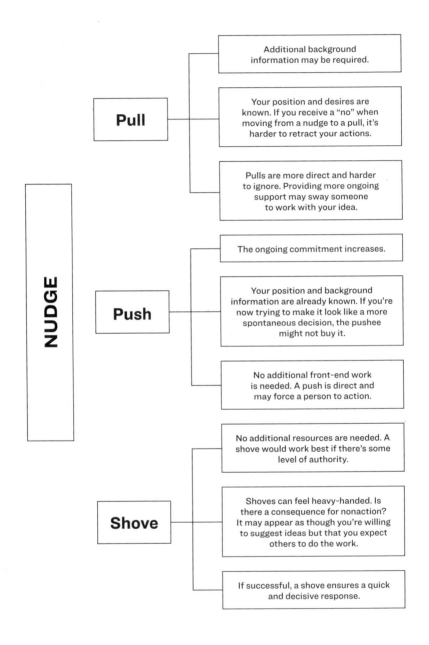

Nudge

As a math coach, I would like to go to the national math conference and have my district approve the days I'll need to take off work, as well as pay for travel. I started mentioning the conference to my administrator, sharing flyers and resources from the sponsoring organization throughout the year. I make sure to mention my desire to go to the conference when my administrator is in meetings with me, but so far she hasn't noticed.

Pull

I research the conference costs and travel information. In a coaches' meeting with our entire team, I then share the group discount. I suggest that a group of our coaching team attends and shares what we learn in professional development offerings when we return.

I may need to research travel costs, hotels, and any additional funds required in more detail. I might also need to be willing to compromise and pay for part of the costs.

My administrator could give an outright "no," suggest I cover either the days off or the costs on my own, or send other coaches but not me. I have to commit to presenting when we return.

If my administrator acknowledges that I'm supporting the team, she may be more likely to let me go. My team will feel involved and supported by me.

Push

I go to my administrator and directly ask for the days off and for my expenses to be paid so I can attend the conference. I commit to delivering professional learning and sharing my experiences when I return.

I already have shared the conference information, so I don't need to provide more resources.

There's a risk of receiving an outright "no" from my administrator. My co-coaches could be jealous they aren't included, and I'll have to deliver professional learning when I return.

I will have an immediate answer and be able to attend the conference. My administrator and coworkers will see me as taking initiative, and I won't have to pay for the expenses.

Shove

I can either go around my administrator by asking her boss for permission, or I can take the days off and pay to attend the conference. Both are shoves, but I decide to take the days off and pay my own way.

I don't have to commit to sharing more information or presenting when I return, but I will need to make travel arrangements on my own.

If my boss has reservations about me going, she might be angry that I didn't discuss attendance with her. I'll have to pay for myself and lose some vacation time. My coworkers might see me as unwilling to share.

I get to attend the conference and learn a lot. My administrator sees my commitment to extending my own network and learning.

References

Baker, W. E. (1994). *Networking smart: How to build relationships for personal and organizational success.* New York: McGraw-Hill.

Bass, B., & Riggio, R. (2006). *Transformational leadership.* New York: Psychology Press.

Blue, A. (2016, September 9). *Hope Street Group Fellows convening.* Keynote address presented at From Classroom to the Capitol, Chicago.

Brinson, D., & Steiner, L. (2007). Building collective efficacy: How leaders inspire teachers to achieve [Issue brief]. Washington, DC: Center for Comprehensive School Reform and Improvement.

Brustein, D. (2015, December 25). 9 networking blunders that undermine your reputation. *Entrepreneur.* Retrieved from https://www.entrepreneur.com/article/254259

Burchell, M., & Robin, J. (2011). *The great workplace.* New York: The Great Workplace Institute.

Burley, S., & Pomphrey, C. (2011). *Mentoring and coaching in schools: Collaborative professional learning inquiry for teachers.* New York: Routledge.

Campbell, J. (1949). *The hero with a thousand faces.* Novato, CA: New World Library.

Crum, A. J., Salovey, P., & Achor, S. (2013). Rethinking stress: The role of mindsets in determining the stress response. *Journal of Personality and Social Psychology, 104*(4), 716–733. doi:10.1037/a0031201

Darwall, S. L. (1977). Two kinds of respect. *Ethics, 88*(1), 36–49. doi:10.1086/292054

Desimone, L. (2009). Improving impact studies of teachers' professional development: Toward better conceptualizations and measures. *Educational Researcher, 38*(3), 181–199. Retrieved from http://www.jstor.org/stable/20532527

DeWitt, P. (2012, January 8). The benefits of failure [Blog post]. Retrieved from http://blogs.edweek.org/edweek/finding_common_ground/2012/01/the_benefits_of_failure.html

Gonzalez, J. (2016, July 21). What advice would you give a student teacher? [Blog post]. Retrieved from https://www.cultofpedagogy.com/student-teaching

Goodwin, B. (2018). *Out of curiosity*. Denver, CO: McREL.

Gratton, L., & Erickson, T. J. (2007, November). Eight ways to build collaborative teams. *Harvard Business Review*. Retrieved from https://hbr.org/2007/11/eight-ways-to-build-collaborative-teams

Guskey, T. R. (2002). Professional development and teacher change. *Teachers and Teaching, 8*(3), 381–391. doi:10.1080/135406002100000512

Haddad, L. (2018, February 15). Seeing failure as an opportunity to learn from (and leapfrog into success). *Entrepreneur*. Retrieved from https://www.entrepreneur.com/article/308943

Henson, R. K. (2001). Teacher self-efficacy: Substantive implications and measurement dilemmas. Paper presented at the annual meeting of the Educational Research Exchange, College Station, TX.

Holmes, L. (2017, December 6). 9 things good listeners do differently. *HuffPost*. Retrieved from https://www.huffpost.com/entry/habits-of-good-listeners_n_5668590

Holt-Lunstad, J., Smith, T., & Layton, J. (2010). Social relationships and mortality risk: A meta-analytic review. *PLOS Medicine, 7*(7). doi:10.1371/journal.pmed.1000316

Huseman, R. C., & Lahiff, J. M. (1981). *Business communication: Strategies and skills.* Hinsdale, IL: Dryden Press.

Huston, T. L. (1983). Power. In H. H. Kelley, E. Berscheid, A. Christensen, J. H. Harvey, T. L. Huston, G. Levinger, et al. (Eds.), *Close relationships* (pp. 169–219). New York: W. H. Freeman.

Ibarra, H. (2006). Career change. In J. H. Greenhaus & G. A. Callanan (Eds.), *The encyclopedia of career development* (pp. 77–82). Thousand Oaks, CA: Sage.

Ibarra, H., & Hansen, M. T. (2011, July–August). Are you a collaborative leader? How great CEOs keep their teams connected. *Harvard Business Review, 68.*

Ibarra, H., & Hunter, M. L. (2007). How leaders create and use networks. *Harvard Business Review, 85*(1), 40–47.

Immordino-Yang, M. H., & Damasio, A. (2007). We feel, therefore we learn: The relevance of affective and social neuroscience to education. *Mind, Brain, and Education, 1*(1), 3–10. doi:10.1111/j.1751-228X.2007.00004.x

Johnson, S., Cooper, C., Cartwright, S., Donald, I., Taylor, P., & Millet, C. (2005). The experience of work-related stress across occupations. *Journal of Managerial Psychology, 20*(2), 178–187.

Jones, D. (2015, January 9). The 36 questions that lead to love. *New York Times.* Retrieved from https://www.nytimes.com/2015/01/11/fashion/no-37-big-wedding-or-small.html

Katz, E., & Blumler, J. G. (Eds.). (1974). *The uses of mass communications: Current perspectives on gratifications research.* Beverly Hills, CA: Sage.

Katz, E., & Lazarsfeld, P. (1955). *Personal influence.* New York: Free Press.

Kim, A., & Gonzales-Black, A. (2018). *The new school rules.* Thousand Oaks, CA: Corwin.

Kirby, E. D., Muroy, S. E., Sun, W. G., Covarrubias, D., Leong, M. J., Barchas, L. A., & Kaufer, D. (2013). Acute stress enhances adult rat hippocampal neurogenesis and activation of newborn neurons via secreted astrocytic FGF2. *Elife, 2.* doi:10.7554/eLife.00362.001

Kreitzer, M. (2016). Why personal relationships are important. Retrieved from https://www.takingcharge.csh.umn.edu/why-personal-relationships-are-important

Leung, L., & Wei, R. (2000). More than just talk on the move: Uses and gratifications of the cellular phone. *Journalism & Mass Communication Quarterly, 77*(2), 308–320.

Marzano, R. J., Simms, J. A., Roy, T., Heflebower, T., & Warrick, P. (2013). *Coaching classroom instruction (classroom strategies).* Bloomington, IN: Marzano Research.

Morgan, N. (2015, May 19). Understand the 4 components of influence. *Harvard Business Review.* Retrieved from https://hbr.org/2015/05/understand-the-4-components-of-influence

Noelle-Neumann, E. (1984). *The spiral of silence: Public opinion, our social skin.* Chicago: University of Chicago Press.

Osterman, K. (2000). Students' need for belonging in the school community. *Review of Educational Research, 70*(3), 323–367.

Porath, C. (2014, November 19). Half of employees don't feel respected by their bosses. *Harvard Business Review.* Retrieved from https://hbr.org/2014/11/half-of-employees-dont-feel-respected-by-their-bosses

Putnam, R. T., & Borko, H. (2000). What do new views of knowledge and thinking have to say about research on teacher learning? *Educational Researcher, 29*(1), 4–15.

Reina, D. S., & Reina, M. L. (2007). Building sustainable trust. *OD Practitioner, 39*(1), 36–41. Retrieved from http://reinatrustbuilding.com/wp-content/uploads/2016/02/ODN-Building-Sustainable-Trust-wout-quiz.pdf

Schmoker, M. (2016). *Leading with focus: Elevating the essentials for school and district improvement.* Alexandria, VA: ASCD.

Sivers, D. (2010, February). *How to start a movement* [Video file]. Retrieved from https://www.ted.com/talks/derek_sivers_how_to_start_a_movement

Stone, D., Patton, B., & Heen, S. (1999). *Difficult conversations: How to discuss what matters most.* New York: Penguin Books.

Sunstein, C., & Thaler, R. (2009). *Nudge: Improving decisions about health, wealth, and happiness.* New York: Penguin Books.

Vogler, C. (1992). *The writer's journey: Mythic structure for writers.* Studio City, CA: Michael Wiese Productions.

Weaver, P., & Mitchell, S. (2012). *Lessons for leaders from the people who matter: How employees around the world view their leaders.* Pittsburgh, PA: DDI.

Williams, S. (2004, June 22). Listening effectively. *Leader Letter.* Retrieved from http://www.wright.edu/~scott.williams/LeaderLetter/listening.htm

Zalis, S. (2018, February 23). Forget networking: Relationship building is the best career shortcut. *Forbes.* Retrieved from https://www.forbes.com/sites/shelleyzalis/2018/02/23/forget-networking-relationship-building-is-the-best-career-shortcut/#48b98961bf7d

Index

Note: Page references followed by an italicized *f* indicate information contained in figures.

About the Authors

Fred Ende is the director of Curriculum and Instructional Services for the Putnam/Northern Westchester Board of Cooperative Educational Services (BOCES). He previously served in this same organization as the regional science coordinator and director of SCIENCE 21. Before that, he worked for 10 years as a middle school science teacher and department chair in Chappaqua, New York. He is one of ASCD's emerging leaders and currently is a board member in ASCD's Emerging Leader Affiliate. He has written and reviewed manuscripts for the National Science Teachers Association (NSTA) and ASCD and has been both a national and regional presenter for both associations. He is an avid writer who blogs monthly for *SmartBrief* and has also written for *Edutopia* and his own website (www.fredende.com). Fred is the author of another ASCD book, *Professional Development That Sticks* (2016), which explores strategies that can help design professional learning that makes the most difference for educators. Fred can be reached at fred.ende@hotmail.com.

Meghan Everette is a mathematics coach in the Salt Lake City School District and the executive director of the ASCD Emerging Leader Alumni Affiliate. She was the 2013 Alabama Elementary Teacher of the Year and a 2015–17 Hope Street Group National Teacher Fellow. Meghan codesigned Powered By Teach to Lead Utah; spent six years as a blogger for the Scholastic Top Teaching blog; and taught at George Hall Elementary, a national turnaround model school in Mobile, Alabama. She is currently a board member of both the Utah Council of Teachers of Mathematics (UCTM) and Utah ASCD. She is a Digital Promise Micro-Credential Ambassador and serves on the Council of Chief State School Officers' Teacher Recruitment and Retention Educator Steering Committee. Meghan is currently pursuing her doctorate in Teachers, Schools, and Society at the University of Florida. She can be reached at meghankeverette@gmail.com.

Related Resources

At the time of publication, the following resources were available (ASCD stock numbers appear in parentheses).

Print Products

100+ Ways to Recognize and Reward Your School Staff by Emily E. Houck (#112051)

Committing to the Culture: How Leaders Can Create and Sustain Positive Schools by Steve Gruenert and Todd Whitaker (#119007)

C.R.A.F.T. Conversations for Teacher Growth: How to Build Bridges and Cultivate Expertise by Sally J. Zepeda, Lakesha Robinson Goff, and Stefanie W. Steele (#120001)

Design Thinking for School Leaders: Five Roles and Mindsets That Ignite Positive Change by Alyssa Gallagher and Kami Thordarson (#118022)

Facilitating Teacher Teams and Authentic PLCs: The Human Side of Leading People, Protocols, and Practices by Daniel R. Venables (#117004)

Leading Change Together: Developing Educator Capacity Within Schools and Systems by Eleanor Drago-Severson and Jessica Blum-DeStefano (#117027)

Never Underestimate Your Teachers: Instructional Leadership for Excellence in Every Classroom by Robyn R. Jackson (#110028)

For up-to-date information about ASCD resources, go to www.ascd.org. You can search the complete archives of *Educational Leadership* at www.ascd.org/el.

ASCD myTeachSource®

Download resources from a professional learning platform with hundreds of research-based best practices and tools for your classroom at http://myteachsource.ascd.org/.

For more information, send an e-mail to member@ascd.org; call 1-800-933-2723 or 703-578-9600; send a fax to 703-575-5400; or write to Information Services, ASCD, 1703 N. Beauregard St., Alexandria, VA 22311-1714 USA.